FOCUS ON SUCCESS

Allgemeine Ausgabe

Workbook

Baden-Württemberg

5th edition

von
Michael Benford
Michael Macfarlane
Isobel Williams

unter Mitarbeit der Verlagsredaktion

Vokabeltrainer-App

*Verfügbar für: iOS, Android
und Windows Phone*

FOCUS ON SUCCESS
Allgemeine Ausgabe
Baden-Württemberg

Verfasser/innen:	Michael Benford, Bochum
	Michael Macfarlane, Oxford
	Isobel Williams, Berlin
Projektleitung:	Andreas Goebel
Verlagsredaktion:	Kari-ann Warnakulasuriya
Außenredaktion:	Katinka Welz, Ingolstadt
Redaktionelle Mitarbeit:	Elise Nelson
Umschlaggestaltung:	Klein & Halm Grafikdesign, Berlin
Layout und technische Umsetzung:	Oxana Rödel, Absatz DTP-Service, Teltow
Coverfoto:	Shutterstock / alice-photo
Illustrationen:	Oxford Designers & Illustrators

Erhältlich sind auch:

Schülerbuch	ISBN 978-3-06-451089-0
Handreichungen zum Unterricht mit Unterrichtsmanager (UM) und 3 Audio-CDs	ISBN 978-3-06-451091-3
Unterrichtsmanager Premium (DVD)	ISBN 978-3-06-451092-0
Vocabulary practice book	ISBN 978-3-06-451079-1
Vokabeltrainer-App für Android, Apple und Windows	im jeweiligen App-Store

Soweit in diesem Lehrwerk Personen fotografisch abgebildet sind und ihnen von der Redaktion fiktive Namen, Berufe, Dialoge und Ähnliches zugeordnet oder diese Personen in bestimmte Kontexte gesetzt werden, dienen diese Zuordnungen und Darstellungen ausschließlich der Veranschaulichung und dem besseren Verständnis des Inhalts.

www.cornelsen.de

Die Webseiten Dritter, deren Internetadressen in diesem Lehrwerk angegeben sind, wurden vor Drucklegung sorgfältig geprüft. Der Verlag übernimmt keine Gewähr für die Aktualität und den Inhalt dieser Seiten oder solcher, die mit ihnen verlinkt sind.

1. Auflage, 5. Druck 2021

Alle Drucke dieser Auflage sind inhaltlich unverändert und können im Unterricht nebeneinander verwendet werden.

Druck: Athesiadruck GmbH

ISBN 978-3-06-451090-6

PEFC zertifiziert
Dieses Produkt stammt aus nachhaltig bewirtschafteten Wäldern und kontrollierten Quellen.
www.pefc.de

PEFC™
PEFC/18-31-166

CONTENTS

FOUNDATION COURSE

1	The cult of celebrity	4
2	The world of sport	7
3	Fashion and brand power	10
4	Leisure and free time	13

MAIN COURSE

5	The virtual world	16
6	Advertising	20
7	Family and beyond	24
8	Entering the world of work	28
9	Multiculturalism	32
10	Helping others	36
11	Global reach	40
12	Changing society	44

EXAM PREPARATION

13	The challenges of the modern state	48
14	Energy and the environment	52
15	Feeding the world	56
16	Technology	60

1 The cult of celebrity

1 TALKING ABOUT CELEBRITY

Underline twelve English words you can use when you talk about celebrities. The words are all on pages 6 and 7 of the student's book.

UPFFANSMXOPAPARAZZIGRLFAMOUSTSTATUSYSTARPLUXURYMLLEGENDZUSTALKERPKACTORMIMAGELBKMAUTOGRAPHCPOPULARITY

2 GETTING IT RIGHT

→ Position of adverbs of time, SB S. 272

Choose the correct position (A or B) for the adverb of time in the brackets.

1 John **A** spends too much money **B** on fan articles. (always)
2 The paparazzi **A** wait for celebrities **B** outside clubs and bars. (usually)
3 **A** I **B** read about celebrities' problems in the newspapers. (regularly)
4 My favourite singer **A** performs **B** in my town. (never)
5 The group is **A** on the radio **B**. (every day)
6 Celebrities **A** love to see their name in the news **B**. (usually)
7 Paparazzi **A** get very rich **B** with their photos. (sometimes)
8 Some stars **A** are **B** on tour. (always)

3 GETTING IT RIGHT

→ Simple present, SB S. 248

Complete the story using the verbs in brackets in the simple present. Take care with questions and negatives.

Briony and Holly Banks ___are___ ¹ (be) twins. They both _____ ²

(love) to dance and they _____ ³ (have) a lot of talent. They

_____ ⁴ (enter) a talent show competition.

On the night of the show, Briony _____ ⁵ (see) that her sister

_____ ⁶ (not be happy). 'What _____ ⁷ (be)

the problem, Holly?' she _____ ⁸ (ask). 'I _____ ⁹

(be scared),' Holly _____ ¹⁰ (tell) her.

When the girls _____ ¹¹ (come) on stage, one of the judges

_____ ¹² (smile) kindly. 'Just _____ ¹³ (relax),' he _____ ¹⁴ (say). Holly suddenly _____ ¹⁵

(feel) great and she and her sister _____ ¹⁶ (win) the competition.

4 ASKING QUESTIONS

→ Simple present, SB S. 248; Question words, SB S. 222

Read the answers a celebrity fashion model gave during a TV interview in London. Use the correct forms of *be* and *do* together with the question words from the box to complete the interviewer's questions. Use each question word only once.

How ▪ What ▪ When ▪ Where ▪ Who ▪ Why

1 _____ your name?   *My name is Willow.*

2 _____ you from?   *I'm from New York.*

3	_____ you like London?	_I love London._
4	_____ you in London today?	_I'm in London today to model some clothes_
5	_____ you usually start work?	_I usually start work at 6 am._
6	_____ your favourite designer?	_My favourite designer is Marco._

5 BUILDING SKILLS

→ Vorbereitung auf das Lesen, SB S. 214

Before you read the text below, study the clues on the page and then choose the best ending to complete the following statement.

The article is about a celebrity who
a believes the media are always nice to her because she is famous.
b knows from experience that being a celebrity is not always fun.
c pays reporters and paparazzi to give her the attention she wants.

SKILLS CHECKLIST: Predicting

☑ Have I read the title?
☑ Have I looked at the photo?
☑ Have I read the caption under the photo?

FAME – IS IT WORTH IT?

A lot of stories about Desirée, last month's winner of _Stars for Tomorrow_, are appearing in the tabloid newspapers at the moment. Talking openly to _Fame and Fortune_ magazine, the slim, sexy singer explains why media attention is not always a good thing.

5 'Everybody is talking about my relationship with Patrick Strong, one of the judges on the show,' she says. 'I know that when you're a celebrity, you have to give up a lot of your private life. The fans want to know what you're doing,' she says. 'Sometimes things appear in the papers that you don't like, but you learn to accept it. Say you're having a bad day, and
10 someone takes your picture and sells it to the media, that's part of the life of a celebrity,' she continues.

'Some of the stories appearing in the press at the moment are just too personal, though. Now that Patrick and I are close, I'm scared to leave the house because I know the reporters and the paparazzi are
15 waiting for me. They are making my life hard at the moment.'

(182 words)

'You know that the media is interested in your private life when you're a celebrity, but I did not expect it to be this bad.'

6 LOOKING AT THE TEXT

→ Rezeption: Leseverstehen, SB S. 214

Say if these statements are true (T) or false (F). Explain your answers.

1 Desirée is currently appearing in _Stars for Tomorrow_.
☐ _____
_____
_____

2 Desirée knows Patrick well because he is her cousin.
☐ _____
_____
_____

3 Desirée understands that her fans are interested in her.
☐ _____
_____
_____

4 She does not want paparazzi to take photos when she is looking bad.

☐ _____

_____

_____

5 The media is full of reports about Desirée's professional plans at the moment.

☐ _____

_____

_____

6 Desirée is unhappy about the attention the press is giving her at the moment.

☐ _____

_____

_____

7 GETTING IT RIGHT

→ Present progressive, SB S. 248

A Complete the transcript of a phone call between Desirée and Patrick with the words and phrases in brackets. Put the verbs in the present progressive.

Desirée Hi Patrick.

Patrick Hi Desirée. I ___*am calling*___ ¹ (call) from my car. What _____² (you do) at the moment?

Desirée I _____³ (read) the latest report about us in the newspaper.

Patrick What story _____⁴ (the press make up) now?

Desirée That you _____⁵ (date) another woman.

Patrick These people _____⁶ (go too far). _____⁷ (they try) to split us up?

Desirée I suppose they _____⁸ (only do) their job. Oh, no! Two reporters _____⁹ (walk up) the path to the front door.

Patrick Don't worry, darling. I _____¹⁰ (drive into) your street right now. I can see them.

B Listen and check.

8 GETTING IT RIGHT

→ Simple present ■ Present progressive, SB S. 248

Choose the simple present or the present progressive to complete the extract from Desirée's fan blog.

I *work / am working* ¹ on a new album and everything *goes / is going* ² well at the moment. OK, I *have / am having* ³ some trouble with the press. The paparazzi *stalk / are stalking* ⁴ me from morning till night and some reporters *look / are looking* ⁵ in the window right now. So what? I *know / am knowing* ⁶ that none of you *believe / are believing* ⁷ the stories in the papers. I *love / am loving* ⁸ you all.

Desirée ♥

---

1 TALKING ABOUT SPORT

A Unscramble the letters to make words and expressions to talk about sport. Some letters have already been given. All the words and expressions are on page 12 of the student's book.

#	Scramble	Answer grid
1	cipainpratt	P · R · · C · · · T
2	acesportt	· · E · T · · · R
3	labofolt	· O · · · A · ·
4	alpy nestin	· · A · · · N · ·
5	proustp a meat	· · · P · · · · A · · E · ·
6	peek-ift avicetisit	· · E · - · · · · A · · · · · · T · · S
7	od cabeiors	· O · · R · · C ·
8	og gigjong	· · · · O · · · G

B Complete the dialogue with six of the words/expressions.

A Hello, Ben. I haven't seen you for ages. How are you? You look very well. Do you still do your

_____¹?

B Yes. I _____² at the gym twice a week and I _____³

in the park every morning. I took part in a charity run last Saturday. That's the first time I've been a

_____⁴ in an event like that. It was a lot of fun. But what about you? You used

to be very keen on _____⁵. Do you still play for a team?

A No. I sometimes kick a ball around with my mates, but I stopped playing seriously ages ago. I still

go to matches, but I'm only a _____⁶ these days. I prefer to watch other people

doing the hard work.

2 GETTING IT RIGHT

→ Simple past, SB S. 250

Complete the sentences with the simple past form of the underlined verb. Be careful with irregular forms.

1 I normally go to the gym twice a week. Last week, I only _____ once.

2 We usually play tennis outside. Yesterday, we _____ in the hall.

3 The team doesn't often win their matches, but they _____ last Saturday.

4 The match usually begins at 3 pm but last week it _____ at 3.30 pm.

5 Where did you buy your running shoes? I _____ them at RunFast.

6 Did you take part in the event this year? Yes. I _____ as usual.

3 GETTING IT RIGHT

→ Present perfect, SB S. 252

A Use the correct form of the verb in brackets to complete the sentences. Circle the signal words.

1 Claire _has left_ ¹ (leave) our swimming club. She _____² (just move) to

another town.

2 Paul _____¹ (not arrive) yet. He _____²

(never be) late for a game before.

3 _____[1] (you / hear) the news already? Mark Miller _____

_____[2] (just join) our local ice hockey team.

4 _____[1] (you / meet) our new player, Jan, yet? She _____[2]

(play) squash in competitions all over the country.

B Complete the expressions with *for* or *since*. → *For, since*, SB S. 253

1 _____ six years 5 _____ last week

2 _____ a long time 6 _____ we moved to Berlin

3 _____ Easter 7 _____ 21 June

4 _____ a couple of hours 8 _____ ever

4 GETTING IT RIGHT

→ Simple past ▪ Present perfect, SB S. 253

Cross out the incorrect version of the verb to complete the text. Circle the expressions that helped you decide. The first one has been done for you.

(Earlier today), the Anti-Doping Agency charged / has charged[1] another sports personality with using performance-enhancing drugs. Up till now, the agency did not say / has not said[2] who the celebrity sportsperson is. According to an insider, however, people from the agency searched / have searched[3] the home of one of the country's top runners earlier this week.

The runner, who won / has won[4] a lot of prizes during his career, told / has told[5] us in a telephone interview yesterday, that he and another runner only drank / have drunk[6] a fruit juice before the event. The fruit-juice company sponsored / has sponsored[7] both runners for over two years. This morning, in a press conference, a spokesperson for the company said / has said[8]: 'Doping in sport was / has been[9] a problem for years but the drinks we gave / have given[10] the runners before the race were / have been[11] pure fruit juice, as always. None of our drinks ever contained / have ever contained[12] drugs.'

5 GETTING IT RIGHT

→ Pronouns, SB S. 267

A Complete each message using a subject or an object pronoun for the underlined words.

EXAMPLE: There is a message from your parents on the answering machine.
Can you listen to ___*it*___ and call ___*them*___ back?

1 Joe is working late and can't come to football practice.

Can you call _____ at the office?

2 I am playing in a hockey team at the moment.

Would you like you to watch _____ play?

3 Clara knows you have some new tennis balls.

_____[1] would like to borrow _____[2].

4 We have a problem with the CD player.

Can you help _____[1] fix _____[2]?

5 Some people say that Zumba is fun. Jessica and I are going to try Zumba.

_____[1] say that Zumba is fun. _____[2] are going to try _____[3].

B Read Ann's blog post about her dance class and find the pronouns. Highlight the subject pronouns in yellow, the object pronouns in green and the possessive adjectives in blue. The first three have been done for you. Now you only have to find 22 more.

Here's some news about my dance class. We have a new instructor. Her name is Alice. She's a really good teacher. Dancing is a great way to keep fit and have fun. It's also a great way to meet people. There are ten of us in the class. A few weeks ago, a boy called Tim had a
5 problem with one of his shoes. Its *sole* [Sohle] broke and this made him fall and crash into me. Those of you who follow this blog know that I've always liked him, but this was the first time he noticed me. It wasn't long till we started going out. His parents have invited us to visit them next weekend in their new home. They have just moved to Glasgow.
10 If you want to join the dance class, send me your email address.

6 BUILDING SKILLS

→ Rezeption: Hörverstehen, SB S. 225

A You are going to listen to three people talk about how they keep fit. Before you listen, look at the photos and study the questions on the notepad below. Then choose the expressions from this list that you think you will hear.

> **SKILLS CHECKLIST: Preparing to listen**
>
> ☑ Have I read the task?
> ☑ Have I studied the questions?
> ☑ Have I thought about the words I might hear?

1 strengthens the heart and the lungs
2 no fun at all
3 reduce stress
4 a fun way to keep fit
5 exercise every bit of your body
6 get slim and stay slim
7 it's really boring
8 helps you relax
9 gives you a good feeling

   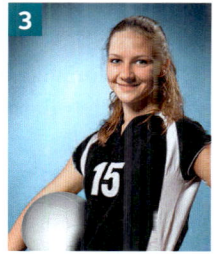

Jane, 26, teacher *Will, 22, trainee* *Lily, 18, student*

Who	What?	Where?	Health benefits?	Other?
Jane, 26, teacher	_____ _____ 1	in class; at _____ 2	good for _____, _____ 3, muscles; gets rid of _____ 4	fun; not _____ 5
Will, 22, trainee	_____ _____ 1	_____ _____ 2	great _____ 3; relaxing / you _____ 4; losing _____ 5	swimming helps you get _____ _____ 5
Lily, 18, student	_____ _____ 1	_____ 2	even if you _____ 3 you feel great; _____ 4 the calories; working with _____ 5 = good feeling	team sport good way to _____ 6; made _____ 7

B Now listen and check.
3

C Before you listen again, use information from the page to fill in the notepad with as much information as you can. Then listen again and complete the notes.
3

> **SKILLS CHECKLIST: Taking notes**
>
> ☑ Have I structured my notes?
> ☑ Have I focused on the task?
> ☑ Have I noted the key information?

3 Fashion and brand power

1 TALKING ABOUT BRANDS

A Translate the words into English to complete the crossword with words you can use to talk about brands. All the words are on pages 18 and 19 of the student's book.

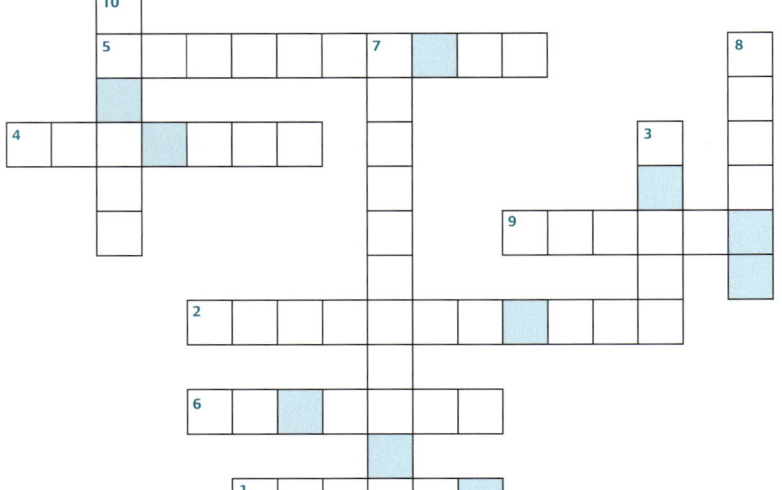

ACROSS:
1 Werbespruch
2 modisch
4 Ware
5 erschwinglich
6 Qualität
9 Wahl

DOWN:
3 Preis
7 Werbung
8 Werte
10 berühmt

B Unscramble the highlighted letters in the crossword to make a two-word expression which says what shoppers often look for.

☐☐☐☐☐ ☐☐☐☐☐

2 GETTING IT RIGHT

→ Adjectives ■ Adverbs of manner, SB S. 269

A Adjective or adverb? Underline the correct form.

1 If you don't have much money, you have to shop careful / carefully.
2 Don't simple / simply buy something because it's been advertised by a star.
3 The clothes look beautiful / beautifully when they're on a model.
4 It is usual / usually safer to buy a brand-name computer.
5 These jeans look similar / similarly to the ones I saw advertised last week.
6 Expensive / expensively products don't always last longer than goods you buy cheap / cheaply.

B Underline the adverbs below then unscramble the words to make sentences. Make sure you put the adverbs in the correct positions.

1 at the outlet store / frequently / Lucy / shops

_____

2 always / dresses / Jim / well

_____

3 my new computer / stopped / suddenly / working

_____

4 good / in that café / is / the coffee / usually

_____

5 I / these boots / really / want

_____

3 USING A DICTIONARY

→ Ein Wörterbuch benutzen, SB S. 217; Vokabeln lernen, SB S. 220

Complete the table using your dictionary. The words are from page 19 of the student's book.

Noun	Verb	Adjective
choice	_____ 1	_____ 2
cost	_____ 3	_____ 4
_____ 5	_____ 6	affordable

4 GETTING IT RIGHT

→ Comparison of adjectives and adverbs, SB S. 270

A Joe is shopping for a new smartphone. Use information from the table to complete his thoughts with the correct form of the words in brackets. Add *as … as* or *… than* where necessary.

	Universe	NeatPhone	Bright
dimensions	142mm × 73mm × 8.1mm	124mm × 59mm × 7.6mm	160mm × 84mm × 8.4mm
weight	145gr	112gr	206gr
battery life	+++++	+++	++++
price	€650	€600	€585

Oh, dear. I'm not sure which of these three phones to choose. I can see that the Universe is _bigger than_ [1] (big) the NeatPhone and the Bright is the _biggest_ [2] (big) of all three, but I'll have to think some more. How heavy are they? The NeatPhone is _____ [3] (light) the two other phones. The Universe is not _____ [4] (heavy) the Bright. The Bright is _____ [5] (heavy) the other two.

What does it say here about the battery life? The battery life of the NeatPhone is not _____ [6] (long) the battery life of the Bright. It looks as if the batteries of the Universe last _____ [7] (long).

What about the price? Well, the Bright is the _____ [8] (cheap) of the phones. The NeatPhone is _____ _____ [9] (expensive) the Bright, and the Universe is the _____ [10] (expensive) of them all. Oh, I don't know which of these three phones is _____ [11] (good). Choosing a phone is one of the _____ [12] (difficult) things to do in life. Hmmm. I think I'll buy the …

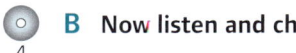

B Now listen and check.

C Listen again. Which phone does Joe choose and why?

5 COLLOCATIONS

→ Ein Wörterbuch benutzen, SB S. 217

Cross out the word which you cannot use to form a collocation with the word in capital letters.

1 current ▪ high ▪ latest ▪ low ▪ newest FASHION
2 famous ▪ leading ▪ popular ▪ victim ▪ well-known BRAND
3 best ▪ good ▪ poor ▪ new ▪ top QUALITY
4 blue ▪ copies ▪ designer ▪ skinny ▪ tight JEANS
5 DESIGNER clothes ▪ house ▪ jeans ▪ label ▪ name

6 BUILDING SKILLS

→ Interaktion: An Diskussionen teilnehmen, SB S. 246

A **How good is your knowledge of phrases for discussion? Without checking the back flap of the student's book, write at least one phrase for each heading.**

SKILLS CHECKLIST: Phrases for discussions

☑ Have I learned suitable phrases for discussion?
☑ Do I know how and when to use them?

Giving an opinion	Giving reasons	Agreeing with an opinion

Disagreeing with an opinion	Interrupting

B **Circle the correct word in brackets to complete the sentences.**

1 My own (reason / view) of the matter is that it's fun to wear the latest fashions.
2 In my (meaning / opinion), the style doesn't suit everyone.
3 The main (reason / idea) is that the clothes are too expensive for teenagers.
4 I'm sorry, but I have to (agree / disagree) with you on that point. Expensive T-shirts don't always last longer than cheap ones.
5 I'm (afraid / concerned) I can't accept that. A designer watch will last forever.
6 Can I just (interrupt / tell) you for a moment? I strongly (agree / believe) that you have to spend money to look good.

C **Imagine that you are going to take part in a discussion about whether to buy designer or regular jeans and why. Complete the cards with arguments for and against designer jeans and regular jeans.**

Designer jeans		Regular jeans	
for	**against**	**for**	**against**
fit better, …	expensive, …	inexpensive, …	poor quality, …
_____	_____	_____	_____
_____	_____	_____	_____
_____	_____	_____	_____
_____	_____	_____	_____

D **Now decide on your point of view and make some notes that you could use in a discussion on the question.**

SKILLS CHECKLIST: Group discussions

☑ Have I thought about what I want to say?
☑ Have I prepared some bullet points?
☑ Have I written down key phrases in English?

Jeans are jeans. The only difference is the name.

Designer jeans last longer and fit better.

E **If you have the chance, carry out the discussion with two or three other people. Check with your teacher if you can do this in class.**

1 TALKING ABOUT FREE TIME ACTIVITIES

Complete the mindmap with free time activities.

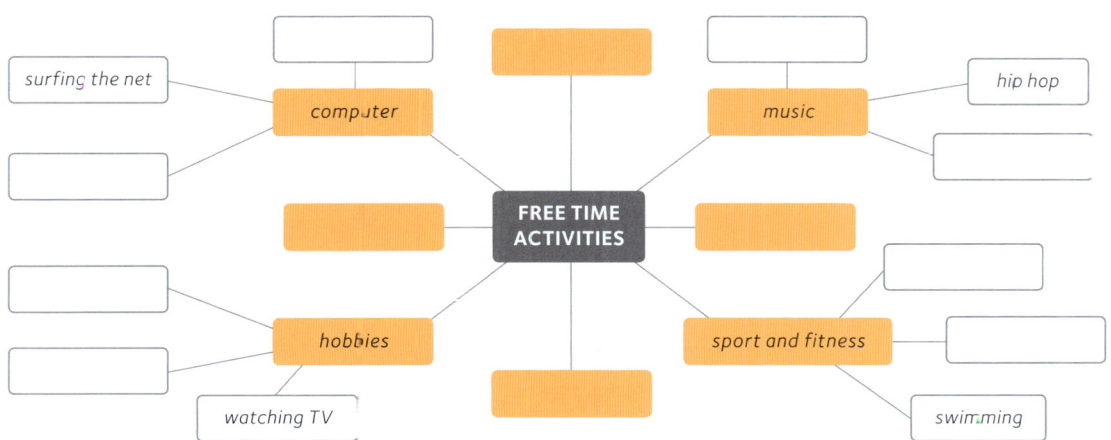

2 GETTING IT RIGHT

→ *Will* future ▪ *Going to* future, SB S. 256

A Fill in the correct form of the *will* future

1 **A** _____¹ (you come) with me to the pop festival tomorrow?

   B Probably not. The weather reporter said there _____² (probably be) a storm in the evening.

   A Oh, no! I hope it _____³ (not be) stormy. If it is, the organizers

   _____⁴ (cancel) the festival.

2 **A** It's disco night at the youth club. _____⁵ (I see) you there later?

   B No, I _____⁶ (not have) time this evening. I have to do my homework.

   A Come on! I _____⁷ (help) you. Then we _____⁸ (be able to) go together.

B Use the notes to make sentences using the *going to* future.

EXAMPLE: Jane / join / salsa class / this winter   *Jane is going to join a salsa class this winter.*

1 I / train for / next marathon

   _____

2 Mark and Mindy / go backpacking / Australia / next summer

   _____

3 some pupils / start / film club / next term

   _____

4 snooker championships / be held / Paris / this year

   _____

5 you / really / buy / motorbike?

   _____

6 I / not go shopping / for the rest of the year

   _____

3 **BUILDING SKILLS**   → Produktion: Cartoons beschreiben und analysieren, SB S. 236

A **Choose the correct words from the brackets to complete the description of the cartoon.**

The cartoon shows a teenage boy and his mother in a living room. The boy _____ [1] (is lying / lies) on the sofa. He _____ [2] (has / is) overweight. He _____ _____ [3] (is looking / looks) frightened because a group of *vultures* [Geier] _____ [4] (are watching / watch) him _____ [5] (hungry / hungrily). Through the open window, we can see that two more vultures _____ [6] (fly / are flying) to join their friends. The boy's mother _____ [7] (stands / is standing) behind her son. She appears to be _____ [8] (angry / angrily). She _____ [9] (shouts / is shouting) the words that are written under the cartoon.

"Maybe if you showed some sign of life once in a while this sort of thing wouldn't happen."

B **Complete the interpretation of the cartoon with one of the sentence endings below.**

The joke is that …
a mothers don't understand anything about relaxing.
b some kids are so lazy that they appear to be dead.
c some vultures have come to eat an overweight boy.

SKILLS CHECKLIST: Interpreting a cartoon

☑ Have I read the caption?
☑ Have I described everything in the cartoon?
☑ Have I used the present progressive to describe what is happening?

4 **LOOKING AT THE TEXT**   → Rezeption: Leseverstehen, SB S. 214

Jenny, 16, often uses her blog to talk about her problems with her parents.

Read the post and say if the following statements are true (T) or false (F).

1 Jenny enjoys listening to how her parents behaved when they were teenagers. ☐

2 She doesn't use any social networks. ☐

3 She likes to meet her friends outside after school. ☐

4 According to Jenny, you can find out about a lot of things on the Internet. ☐

5 She doesn't want to have contact with people online. ☐

6 She would like the older generation to be more tolerant towards teenagers. ☐

'When I was your age …'

How often have you heard this in the last few weeks? You're chilling, lying on the sofa, listening to music or checking some post and – bang! – all the good feelings disappear and you have to listen to how life was in the old days. Everybody wrote letters and if you wanted to chat, you sat on the step and spoke to the kids next door. So what? History is interesting, but things change and develop.   →

5   Kids today use social networking. I don't have to be with my friends in person to have a conversation, I can
    video call them. I don't need go to my mate's house and tell him about a great new band, I can post a link to it
    in our Facebook group.

    It's not all about having fun. We also use social networking to discuss schoolwork and to exchange ideas.
    We are open to other people's ideas and enjoy mixing with people from different groups.

10 I wish people would just understand that things are different today. I mean, when my parents and grandparents
    were growing up they didn't even have computers!

    Perhaps, when older people start a sentence with, 'When I was your age …' they should try to end it with
    the words, 'I was a teenager, too.'   (214 words)

5   BUILDING SKILLS

→ Schriftliche Mediation, SB S. 240

Ein Freund hat Ihnen erzählt, dass seine Mutter ständig
zu ihm sagt: „Als ich in deinem Alter war…!". Schreiben
Sie eine E-Mail an diesen Freund und erzählen Sie ihm
von Jennys Blog aus Übung 4, und erläutern Sie Jennys
Anregungen zu diesem Thema.

SKILLS CHECKLIST: Written mediation

☑ Have I read the situation?
☑ Have I understood who the mediation is for?
☑ Have I written the right sort of text?

6   GETTING IT RIGHT

→ Quantifiers, SB S. 273

Choose the correct words from the brackets to complete the dialogues.

1   A   Did you see _____¹ (any / some) interesting programmes on TV last night?

    B   I don't watch _____² (many / much) TV. I do so many other things and there's too

        _____³ (few / little) time to fit everything in.

2   A   I go to the gym _____⁴ (a few / a little) times a week. What about you?

    B   I go to the gym, too. There are often _____⁵ (any / some) interesting people there.

3   A   Does your college offer _____⁶ (many / much) after-school activities?

    B   No, they don't offer _____⁷ (any / some). Not _____⁸ (many / much) people

        are interested.

4   A   We have _____⁹ (a few / a little) time before the dance class starts. Can you show me

        _____¹⁰ (any / some) moves?

    B   If you like. How _____¹¹ (many / much) moves do you know already?

    A   Not _____¹² (many / much). I've only been here _____¹³ (a few / a little) times and

        I don't practise _____¹⁴ (many / much) at home.

7   BUILDING SKILLS

→ Produktion: Bilder beschreiben und analysieren, SB S. 236

**Describe the photo, relating it to the topic of the unit.
Explain why you would (not) enjoy the activity shown.**

SKILLS CHECKLIST: Describing a picture

☑ Have I described the people in the picture?
☑ Have I described the atmosphere?

1 WORKING WITH WORDS

Fill in the gaps with some of the highlighted words from the text on pages 36 and 37 of the student's book.

_____[1] of how old you are – you can be a child or an _____[2] –

you're never too old to open a social media account. There are _____[3] to choose from,

e.g. Facebook, Twitter, LinkedIn or Instagram. At first sight they _____[4] to be very different,

but they are the same in many ways. This is because they let people _____[5] with each other

and help them feel less cut off and _____[6].

A recent _____[7] conducted by an online bank has shown that on _____[8], Britons

spend at least one hour on the Internet per day. In some cases, the amount of time spent on social media

_____[9] two hours. For these reasons, many people open a social media account to

_____[10] being forgotten by their friends.

2 BUILDING SKILLS

→ Rezeption: Leseverstehen – Grobverständnis, SB S. 214

A **Study the box on the right then skim the text and decide which of the following statements best summarizes it.**

a Social media only played a small part in the volunteers' lives.
b Only the lonely use Facebook and Twitter.
c Giving up social media can make room for other things.
d Social media use is a bad habit that must be broken.

SKILLS CHECKLIST: Skimming
☑ Have I read the title carefully?
☑ Have I read all of the first paragraph?
☑ Have I read the first sentence of all the other paragraphs?
☑ Have I read all of the final paragraph?

B **Read the text again and make a list of the following:**

1 the withdrawal symptoms people felt
2 the things that some people started to do again

FACEBOOK AND TWITTER ADDICTS GO 'COLD TURKEY' IN MAJOR EXPERIMENT

The research project focused on a month-long experiment where 40 people from across the UK were forced to change their normal social media behaviours. A number of Facebook and Twitter _addicts_ suffered a range of _withdrawal symptoms_ after being forced to deactivate their accounts for a month.

5 Many described extreme feelings of isolation because of the reduced contact with friends or family, while others said they were frustrated at losing their key communication tool. Some users lost contact with friends and family because they had no contact details other than a Facebook address.

As one female _volunteer_ from Yorkshire _admitted_: 'So much of my life was organised via Facebook. I haven't communicated with my family all week.' Another of the volunteers said: 'I've 10 felt alone and cut off from the world. My fingers seem to be programmed to seek out the Facebook app every time I pick up my phone.'

Social media addicts had to find other ways to spend their time. A woman from Wales said being taken off Facebook had allowed her to focus on the household, while another volunteer _confessed_ the 'ban' had allowed her to spend more time with her daughter. (195 words)

Vocabulary notes					
cold turkey	_kalter Entzug_	withdrawal symptoms	_Entzugserscheinungen_	to admit	_zugeben_
addict	_Süchtige(r)_	volunteer	_Freiwillige(r)_	to confess	_gestehen_

3 **GETTING IT RIGHT** → Simple past, SB S. 250

Put the underlined verbs into the simple past. Use the list of irregular verbs on page 342 of the student's book to help you.

SARAH GETS A SHOCK

Sarah goes _____¹ online, opens _____² her Facebook account and

checks _____³ her messages. She finds _____⁴ one with a picture of

herself at a party and is _____⁵ shocked. At first, she thinks _____⁶ there is

_____⁷ only one message, but then she finds _____⁸ another and another.

She doesn't _____⁹ know what to do.

At school, she sits _____¹⁰ in the classroom and looks _____¹¹ around her. Are

_____¹² these people her friends or her enemies now? How much do _____¹³ they

know about her? Sarah doesn't _____¹⁴ notice the teacher and can't _____¹⁵

answer his questions. The bell rings _____¹⁶ and the lesson is _____¹⁷ over. Sarah

leaves _____¹⁸ the classroom and understands _____¹⁹ one thing: She

must _____²⁰ tell someone, but who?

---

4 **LISTENING**

5

Eine Mutter, Margaret Green, bringt ihren Sohn zu einer Party, die im Haus der Familie Seale stattfindet, und telefoniert anschließend mit Frau Seale. Hören Sie dem Telefonat aufmerksam zu und entscheiden Sie, ob die unten stehender Aussagen über den Hörtext richtig oder falsch sind. Begründen Sie Ihre Entscheidung auf Deutsch.

EXAM
→ Hörverstehen,
SB S. 178

1 Catherine Seale phones Margaret Green.
2 The two women's sons are in the same class at school.
3 Margaret Green knows that the Seales are on holiday in France.
4 Margaret Green is in the front garden of Catherine's house.
5 Christopher told his mother he planned to throw a party.
6 The party is out of control.
7 The riot police are trying to break into the house through the roof.
8 The riot police are blocking the street.
9 Catherine's son planned to pay a bouncer to make sure only the right guests got in.
10 Mrs Green stopped the people wrecking the front garden.

---

5 **GETTING IT RIGHT** → Simple past ■ Present perfect, SB S. 253

Complete the sentences with the simple past or the present perfect.

1 Sarah (not use) _____ Facebook for over twelve months now.

2 She last (use) _____ it last year.

3 Since then she (change) _____¹ schools and (make) _____²
   new friends.

4 The first few weeks at her new school (not be) _____¹ easy but after a month or

   so she (feel) _____² at home.

5 When she (tell) _____¹ her new friends about the cyberbullying, they (be)

_____² shocked.

6 In the past, Sarah (spend) _____ at least three hours a day online.

7 This year she (not be) _____ online at all.

8 Her life (change) _____ a lot since she started at her new school.

6 **BUILDING SKILLS**

'Should mobiles be banned in schools?'

Write a composition. Use the information from at least three of the materials on the next page. Use the four steps for text production outlined in exercises A–D to help you.

EXAM
→ materialgestützter Aufsatz, SB S. 180

SKILLS CHECKLIST: Text production

☑ Have I chosen at least three materials?
☑ Have I referred to the topic of the essay and discussed various aspects?
☑ Have I summarized the main points and given my opinion?

A Organizing the materials: Decide which of the materials can be used to argue for or against a mobile phone ban and which provide background information.

B Using relevant vocabulary: Complete the statements about all five materials with words from the box.

> access ■ believe ■ chart ■ clearly ■ dependent ■ distract ■
> encourage ■ important ■ message

1 School is a place where people learn, but the _____ of the cartoon is that people

using mobile devices don't think or notice what is going on around them.

2 We can see from the _____¹ that almost 80 per cent of teenagers have a smartphone,

and that the phones are far more _____² to them than a computer or TV.

3 The quote _____¹ shows that people can become emotionally

_____² on electronic media and feel isolated without them.

4 Some teachers _____¹ their pupils to use their smartphones for schoolwork and home

learning. The pupils can _____² the data they need from anywhere and at any time.

5 Other teachers are against smartphones at school because the phones have too many functions that

_____¹ pupils from their schoolwork. They _____² that mobiles

should be switched off at school.

C Writing whole sentences: Match the words and expressions in the box with the five materials (three for each) and then use them to write one or two sentences about each material.

> a must-have ■ better equipped than many schools ■ mentally distant ■ more/less important than ■
> the minority/majority (+ plural form of the verb) ■ to accompany you everywhere you go ■
> to be distracting/annoying ■ to be in contact with the teachers ■ to be pragmatic/flexible/
> up-to-date/modern ■ to become addicted to ■ to cheat in a class test ■ to feel lost and unhappy
> without it ■ to help you stay in touch with people ■ to neglect your friends ■
> to not notice what is happening around them

D Use some of the words and expressions from exercises A–C together with your own ideas to write your composition. Make sure you state your opinion clearly. The *Language for writing* on the back flap of the student's book may help you.

1

2

Smartphone gehört bei Teenies zur Grundausstattung

Diese elektronischen Geräte besitzen 12- bis 17-Jährige in Deutschland persönlich (in %)

Smartphone mit Internetnutzung	79%
PC (Desktop oder Laptop)	64%
Spielkonsole (stationär oder tragbar	57%
Fernsehgerät	50%
Tablet-Computer	21%
Handy ohne Internet	18%
Keines davon	1%

nach Quelle: *TK/Forsa*

3

'My cell phone is my best friend. It's my lifeline to the outside world.'

Carrie Underwood (American singer, songwriter and actress)

4

Graham Barker, deputy head and head of e-learning, St Julian's School, Newport:

'We lifted the ban on mobile phones last term because we realised that the students had all got powerful computers in their pockets and we just couldn't afford to provide all of them with that
5 level of technology. We needed to take advantage of the fact they all had mobiles.

Obviously, the use of the mobiles is up to each teacher, but we use a cloud-based environment and so the children need to access that. They can
10 do that with their mobile phones at the bus stop, at home, or if they are waiting at school for something.

With our move to the cloud we have got rid of paper-based diaries, and so for their home learning students use their mobile phones. They have an app
15 they use for their timetable. Many of the teachers are also using Twitter to give instructions to students, and that has proved to be very popular.'

From: *The Guardian Online*, 10 September 2012

5

Kerstin Gleine, Friedrich-Ebert-Gymnasium Hamburg, Lehrerin der Jahres 2013 beim Klaus-von-Klitzing-Preis:

"Ja, wenn es sich um Smartphones handelt. Denn: Ein klingelndes Mobiltelefon stört immer den Unterricht. Spiele und Musik auf Smartphones lenken Schüler ab. Schüler können mit Smartphones bei Klassenarbeiten
5 leichter betrügen. Wenn Schüler in den Pausen nur mit ihrem Handy beschäftigt sind, kümmern sie sich nicht mehr um ihre Mitschüler und ihre Beziehungen untereinander. Und: Teure Smartphones sind ein Statussymbol. Einfache Mobiltelefone, mit denen man
10 nur telefonieren beziehungsweise SMS versenden kann, sollten eine Ausnahme sein Sie ermöglichen Schülern einen leichten Kontakt mit ihren Eltern, insbesondere bei längeren Schulwegen. Während der Schulzeit einschließlich der Pausen sollen jedoch auch
15 diese Mobiltelefone unbedingt ausgeschaltet bleiben."

From: *Spiegel Online*, 23 September 2014

WHO SAYS WHAT?

Study the text and the diagram text on page 44 of the student's book and then group the statements under the headings *Natives* and *Immigrants*.

FURTHER OPTIONS

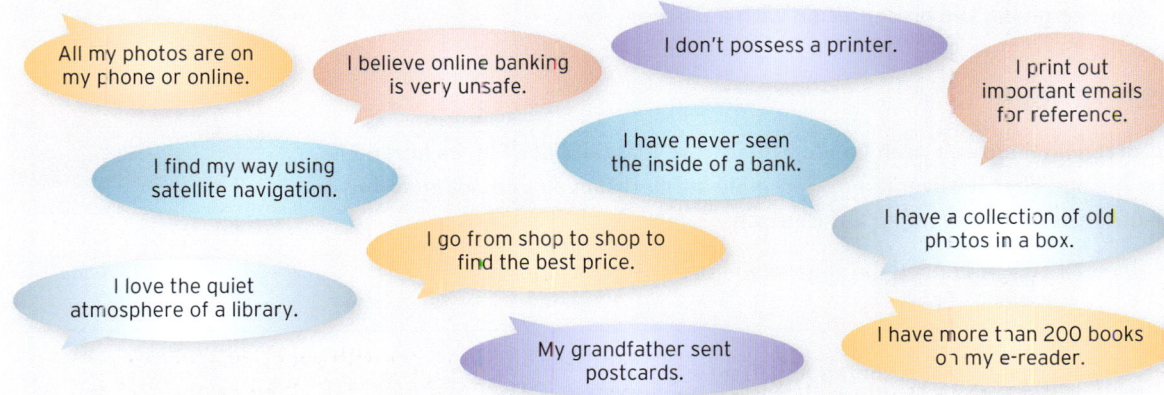

All my photos are on my phone or online.

I believe online banking is very unsafe.

I don't possess a printer.

I print out important emails for reference.

I find my way using satellite navigation.

I have never seen the inside of a bank.

I have a collection of old photos in a box.

I go from shop to shop to find the best price.

I love the quiet atmosphere of a library.

My grandfather sent postcards.

I have more than 200 books on my e-reader.

1 LOOKING AT THE TEXT

→ Rezeption: Leseverstehen, SB S. 214

Look at text A on page 46 of the student's book and then match the sentence halves.

1	VW found that traditional advertising methods	a	use the stairs instead of the escalator.
2	In order to advertise their cars	b	clever, environmentally-friendly technology.
3	VW and their ad agency DDB therefore	c	in Stockholm, Sweden.
4	They started the campaign at a subway station	d	they realised they could play music with them.
5	They wanted to encourage people to	e	were becoming less and less effective.
6	VW made it attractive to use the stairs by	f	it went viral.
7	A lot of commuters chose to use the stairs when	g	VW needed to do something very different.
8	When VW released a video of the musical stairs	h	the public to enter a video competition.
9	After releasing two more viral videos, VW invited	i	invented the 'Fun Theory'.
10	The public now associate VW's cars with	j	making them produce notes like a piano.

2 BUILDING SKILLS

→ Präsentieren, SB S. 243

Sevda and Frank have prepared a presentation on a fun solution to encourage people to wear safety belts in cars. However, their notes have got mixed up.

SKILLS CHECKLIST: Presentations

- ☑ Have I checked the slides?
- ☑ Have I looked at the *Useful phrases*?
- ☑ Have I practised the presentation in my team?

A Look at the *Useful phrases* on page 48 of the student's book and then put the presentation in the right order.

- ☐ **a Frank:** If you have any questions, we'll be pleased to answer them.
- ☐ **b Sevda:** As you can see from this slide, the dummies are injured because they are not wearing seat belts.
- ☐ **c Frank:** So how can we encourage people to wear seat belts? In this slide you can see an in-car entertainment screen for back seat passengers, for example children.
- ☐ **d Sevda:** Good morning. My name's Sevda and this is my colleague Frank.
- ☐ **e Frank:** Thanks for coming to this presentation.
- ☐ **f Sevda:** Today we're going to look at the problem of road safety.
- ☐ **g Frank:** To sum up, this solution makes it fun to be safe.
- ☐ **h Sevda:** In this slide you can see how a car and the passengers look after a car crash. By the way, this one has dummies, not real passengers.
- ☐ **i Sevda:** Let's begin by seeing what happens when a car crashes.
- ☐ **j Sevda:** Frank is now going to talk about a fun solution to make people wear seat belts.
- ☐ **k Frank:** But it only works if you're wearing your seat belt.
- ☐ **l Frank:** Children in the back seat naturally want to use the entertainment system.

B Practise giving the presentation with a partner.

3 LISTENING

Sie sitzen im Flugzeug nach London Heathrow. Während des Fluges hören Sie eine Ansage über Bordverkäufe. Hören Sie aufmerksam zu und beantworten Sie die unten stehenden Fragen auf Deutsch.

EXAM
→ Hörverstehen, SB S. 178

1 Wie viel billiger können die angebotenen Produkte sein?

_____

2 Wie lang gelten die erwähnten Angebote?

_____

3 Welche zwei Produkte werden erwähnt?

_____

4 Zu welchem Preis werden die zwei Produkte jeweils angeboten?

_____

5 Welche Zahlungsmittel werden akzeptiert?

_____

4 **GETTING IT RIGHT**   → *Will* future ▪ *Going to* future, SB S. 256

A **Tom Slater at Ad-Agency Plus in Edinburgh is discussing the launch of a new range of MyStyle wearables. Use the notes to make sentences with the *will* future (predicted actions), the *going to* future (intended actions) or the present progressive (fixed arrangements).**

1 I'm sure / wearables / be / great success / near future (prediction)

_____

2 We / launch / the whole range / in Edinburgh / Monday (fixed arrangement)

_____

3 Each member / my team / demonstrate / different sort of wearable (intended action)

_____

4 I / wear / waterproof Android watch (intended action)

_____

5 We / have / press conference / 9 am (fixed arrangement)

_____

6 We / believe / demand for wearables / double / next six months (prediction)

_____

B **Tom and his team are presenting MyStyle wearables at a big consumer electronics store in Edinburgh. Complete the sentences using the present progressive (fixed arrangements), the *going to* future (intended actions) or the *will* future (predicted actions).**

Good morning and welcome to the launch of MyStyle's range of fantastic new wearables! This morning

_____¹ (introduce) you to a world of clever new products and

we're that sure that _____² (make) your life more fun! _____

_____³ (start) by showing you our Bodylife-tracker model. If you wear a Bodylife-tracker,

_____⁴ (be) able to record your physical, social and entertainment activities 24/7.

Top Olympic athlete Jessi Jones wore one for a whole week, and when you watch the video clip, _____

_____⁵ (see) how it works. We all know that Jessi _____⁶

(compete) for the UK in the World Championships next month. _____⁷ (take)

part in six events and we're certain that _____⁸ (win) six medals, so we at

MyStyle wish her good luck! After the video clip, _____⁹ (ask) you to fill in

postcards, so you can all take part in our 'Good Luck Jessi!' draw. We can tell you now that someone here

today _____¹⁰ (win) a free trip for two to the World Championships next month!

5 BUILDING SKILLS

→ Scannen nach Einzelinformationen im Text, SB S. 221

Study the checklist and then scan the text and answer the questions.

1 When was Sony founded?
2 How many famous new products did Sony bring out bring out between 1955 and 2013?
3 What went wrong in 2011?

SKILLS CHECKLIST: Scanning

☑ Have I read the questions carefully?
☑ Have I focused on one type of information only?

SONY: The history of a household name

Ask anyone what they first think of when they hear the word 'Sony' and each generation will tell you something different. *Depending on* your age, you will say anything *ranging from* the transistor
5 radio (first made by Sony in 1955) to the Trinitron colour TV (1973), the Walkman (1979), the first CD player (1982), the camcorder (1987), the PlayStation (1994), AIBO the robotic dog (1999) or the first waterproof smartphone, tablet
10 computer and smartwatch (2013).

Sony started to think global as early as 1955 when the Tokyo Tsoshiu Kogyo company changed its brand name to Sony. Suddenly everyone was able to *pronounce* the Japanese company's name
15 and the Sony logo started to appear all over the world. In 1961 Sony was also the first Japanese company to sell its *shares* in the US, thereby opening the door to the world's biggest consumer market and preparing the ground for new
20 products.

Since being established by Akio Morita and Masaru Ibuka on 7 May 1946, Sony has con-sistently changed our lifestyles. Radios used to be large pieces of furniture made of wood which
25 people listened to at home. This changed in 1958 when Sony brought out the legendary portable TR-63 shirt pocket transistor radio described as 'the smallest transistor radio in the world'. People could suddenly listen to the radio anywhere they

chose. Up to the end of the 1970s, listening to 30
music had also meant staying in one place because record players, tape recorders and *jukeboxes* were big and heavy. This changed when Sony's *founder*, Masaru Ibuka asked an audio engineer to make him a portable tape player, so he could listen to 35
opera on *long-haul flights* from Japan to the US. The first Walkman was born and Sony kept the name for its MiniDisc (1991), MP3 player (2003) and Android Walkman (2012).

However, it hasn't always been *plain sailing*. 40
Sony's PlayStation network was hacked in 2011 and personal details from 77 million accounts were *compromised*. The company also stopped selling laptops and PCs in 2014 because they were not making a profit.   (343 words) 45

Vocabulary notes

depending on	*je nach*	founder	*Gründer*
ranging from ... to	*von ... über ... bis*	long-haul flight	*Langstreckenflug*
to pronounce	*aussprechen*	plain sailing	*einfach, problemlos*
shares	*Aktien*	compromised	*kompromittiert, nicht mehr sicher*
jukebox	*Musikbox*		

6 MEDIATION

EXAM
→ Mediation, SB S. 179

A **Ihre Schule nimmt am Projekt Zeitung und Schule (Zeus) teil, und Sie sollen einen Beitrag zur Artikelreihe „Erfindungen, die unser Leben verändert haben" schreiben. Sie finden einen Text über Sony im Internet (siehe Übung 5), in dem mehrere Erfindungen erwähnt werden.**

Lesen Sie zuerst den Text über Sony auf Seite 22. Lesen Sie anschließend die acht Sätze unten sorgfältig durch, und ordnen Sie diese den Kategorien *relevant, irrelevant, direkte Übersetzung* und *persönliche Meinung* zu.

1   Das Unternehmen stellte 2014 auch die Produktion von Laptops und PCs ein, weil sie keinen Gewinn erzielten.
2   Der erste Roboterhund wurde genau 20 Jahre nach dem ersten Walkman auf den Markt gebracht.
3   Die wichtigste Erfindung ist der Walkman.
4   Dies änderte sich, als Sony-Gründer Masaru Ibuka einen Toningenieur bat, ihm ein tragbares Tonbandgerät zu bauen, damit er auf Langstreckenflügen von Japan in die USA Oper hören konnte.
5   Es war auf einmal nicht mehr notwendig, an einem Ort zu bleiben, um Radio zu hören.
6   Sony hat mit seinen Erfindungen neue Maßstäbe gesetzt und unser Rezeptionsverhalten stark beeinflusst.
7   Sony hieß früher Tokyo Tsoshiu Kogyo, was schwer auszusprechen war.
8   Geräte von Sony haben ein sehr gutes Preis-Leistungsverhältnis.

B   Schreiben Sie nun den in Teil A erwähnten Zeitungsartikel, in dem Sie schildern, wie Sony zur Veränderung unseres täglichen Lebens beigetragen hat. Benutzen Sie Ihre Antworten aus A als Hilfe.

7   BUILDING SKILLS

→ Produktion: Schaubilder beschreiben und analysieren, SB S. 233

Look at the *Building skills* and *Useful phrases* boxes on pages 52 and 53 of the student's book and then complete the sentences about the graph on page 52. Use the simple present, the present perfect or the simple past.

The graph _____¹ (give) us a clear indication of how media ad spending in the US _____

_____² (increase) every year since 2011. It _____³ (rise) fastest in 2012 but then

_____⁴ (go) up more slowly in 2013. In general, the graph _____⁵ (show) us how,

over the years, spending _____⁶ (rise) by hundreds of millions of dollars every year.

The overall trend _____⁷ (be) still upwards, so we can say that American admen still

_____⁸ (not stop) investing large sums of money in media advertising.

FURTHER OPTIONS

Look at the texts on page 54 of the student's book and then match the words in the box with the definitions in the table. Blue is for Michael Jordan and red is for Kate Moss.

> disappointed ▪ rapidly ▪ huge ▪ achievement ▪ improve ▪ determination ▪ estimate ▪ merchandising ▪ skinny ▪ raw ▪ undernourished ▪ curvaceous ▪ shape ▪ major ▪ immediately ▪ rehab

Michael Jordan	Kate Moss
not giving up when things are hard	at once, without delay
quickly	form, contour
selling goods connected with a famous person or event	in its natural state, unchanged
success	important
to become better	not getting enough to eat
to suggest an amount or a figure without exact data	treatment to stop drug addiction
unhappy because you don't get something you hoped for	very thin
very large	with attractive curves

1 WORKING WITH WORDS

A Match these words from the text on pages 56 and 57 of the student's book to their opposites (1–8).

> borrow ▪ criticize ▪ extended ▪ forget ▪ huge ▪ long-distance ▪ noisy ▪ together

1 lend _____   5 quiet _____

2 local _____   6 remember _____

3 nuclear _____   7 separately _____

4 praise _____   8 tiny _____

B Use pairs of words from part A to complete the following sentences.

1 My grandmother lives nearby in the _____ [1] area but my aunt lives in Australia – that means spending a lot of money on _____ [2] calls!

2 It's too _____ [1] to talk properly here with all the children running around. But it's _____ [2] outside, so let's go out there.

3 **A** Did you _____ [1] to send Grandad's birthday card on the way home?

   B Oh, no, I'm sorry, I _____ [2]. I'll go to the post office now.

4 **A** Are you and your parents going to travel _____ [1]?

   B No, we're going _____ [2]. They're going by train, and I'm flying.

5 Traditionally, people used to live together as part of a large, _____ [1] family, but in the modern world, the small, _____ [2] family unit has become much more common.

6 We'd need a _____ [1] house if the whole family lived together. There isn't enough room for our grandparents in this _____ [2] house!

7 **A** Could I _____ [1] some money for a few days?

   B Well, I can _____ [2] you €50 until Friday, but I'd have to have it back by then.

8 Why do you always _____ [1] the children's school work so much? You need to be more positive and _____ [2] them when they get things right.

2 GETTING IT RIGHT

→ Relative clauses, SB S. 268

A Complete the story with the statements in the box. Change them into relative clauses, using *who* or *which*.

> ▪ They were offered jobs.   ▪ It was very poor.
> ▪ It paid very little.   ▪ He came to England first.
> ▪ He was hiring workers for a UK textile company. ▪ They followed their arrival.
> ▪ He never gave up on anything.   ▪ It would offer a better future.

Rajeev's Grandad Deepak was the one _____ [1].

He and his young wife Mira came from a rural village in northern India _____

_____ [2]. They both had jobs at a local textile workshop _____

_____ [3]. Not surprisingly, they wanted a new life – a life _____

_____ **4**. Then one day the village was visited by an agent

_____ **5**. Deepak and three other men

_____ **6** travelled together to Bradford in the

north of England. The months _____ **7** were

very difficult, but Deepak was a young man _____ **8**.

He worked and saved hard and six months later he was able to bring Mira over from India to join him.

B **Now complete the dialogue with the statements in the box. Change them into relative clauses, leaving out _who_ (or _that_) and _which_ (or _that_) where possible.**

- I've been most worried about them.
- I had to go next.
- She knew she might soon lose it.
- She pushed for us to move here.
- The company had already got rid of them.
- It was doing badly.
- It made us decide to move.
- The EU financial crisis hit it very badly.

One day, Lisa's dad was talking to Tom, a colleague at work.

Tom So tell me, what brought you over to England?

Dad Well, the thing _____ **1** was work. You see,

my wife Kim had a job _____ **2**. As

for me, I worked in Sales for a company _____ **3**.

There were others _____ **4**, and I knew that

I might be the one _____ **5**.

Tom That must have been a very hard time. Ireland was one of the countries _____

_____ **6**, wasn't it?

Dad That's right, but I kept hoping our problems would go away. In the end, it was Kim

_____ **7**.

Tom Are you happy you made the move?

Dad I am now, but it's been hard. It's our children Lisa and Sam _____

_____ **8**. Especially Lisa. She tries to be cheerful, but I know she's often been

lonely. We're all looking forward to seeing all our family again over Christmas

3 **LISTENING**

EXAM
→ Hörverstehen, SB S. 178

Carrie hat ein Gespräch mit einem Sozialarbeiter. Er möchte zunächst ein paar Angaben zu ihrer Person notieren. Hören Sie aufmerksam zu und vervollständigen Sie dann das unten stehende Raster auf Deutsch mit Informationen aus dem Hörtext.

Persönliche Angaben			
Nachname	**1**	Vorname(n)	**2**
Alter	**3**	Geburtsdatum	**4**
Adresse			**5**
Postleitzahl	**6**	Telefonnummer (Handy)	**7**

→ Simple past ▪ Past progressive, SB S. 250

4 GETTING IT RIGHT

Put the verbs in brackets in the simple past or past progressive.

Last year, three friends _____¹ (live) together in a student house. However, they

_____² (not get on) very well because no one _____³ (clean up)

after themselves. They _____⁴ (have) rules about the kitchen, but no one

_____⁵ (keep) to them. One evening they _____⁶ (all cook) at the

same time when they _____⁷ (have) a big argument. It _____⁸

(start) when Ellie _____⁹ (look for) a pan – but they _____¹⁰ (be)

all dirty. Tim _____¹¹ (try) to find some eggs, but when he _____¹²

(open) the fridge, he quickly _____¹³ (have to) shut it again because of the smell. Jamie

_____¹⁴ (look forward) to some soup, but when he _____¹⁵ (look)

in the cupboard it _____¹⁶ (be) all gone. At first they all _____¹⁷

(shout) at each other, but then they _____¹⁸ (agree) to change their ways.

5 TEXT PRODUCTION

'What are the advantages and disadvantages of living in extended families?'

Write a composition. Use the information from at least three of the materials given.

> **EXAM**
> → materialgestützter Aufsatz, SB S. 180

1

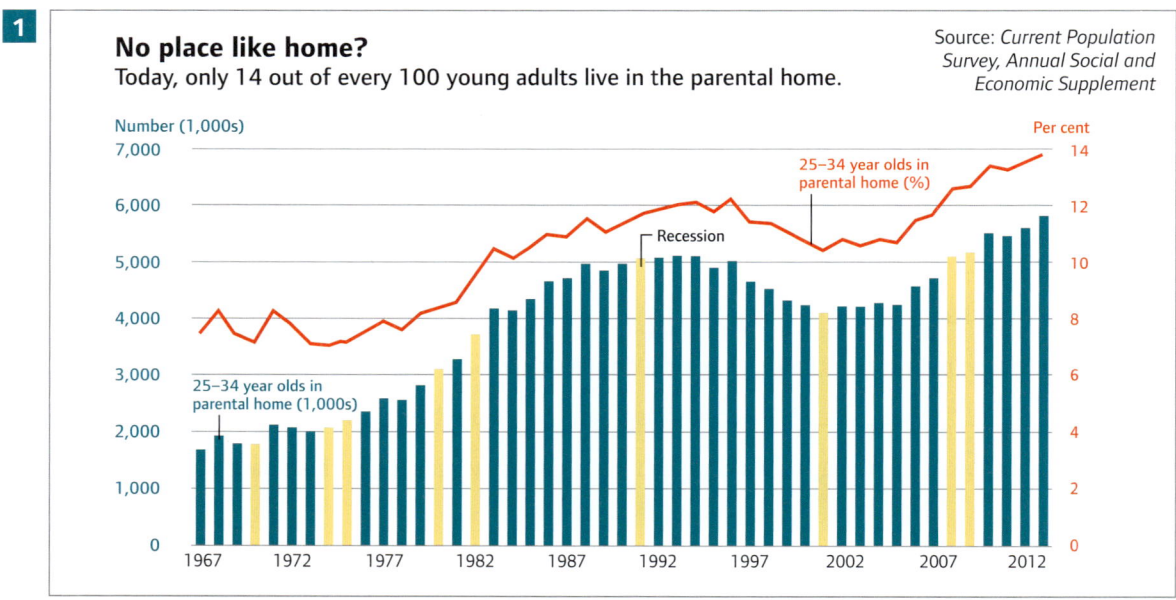

No place like home?
Today, only 14 out of every 100 young adults live in the parental home.

Source: *Current Population Survey, Annual Social and Economic Supplement*

Number (1,000s) — 25–34 year olds in parental home (1,000s) — Recession — 25–34 year olds in parental home (%) — Per cent. Years: 1967, 1972, 1977, 1982, 1987, 1992, 1997, 2002, 2007, 2012.

2

Return of the extended family home as sandwich generation takes in old and young

[...] The effects of recession, property prices and the cost of care for old and young have combined to revive the practice of several generations living under the same roof, research suggests.

Almost 36 million people in Britain now have experience of living as adults in the same home as another generation of their family, the study estimates. [...] It suggests that multi-generational households are becoming the norm. The figure includes the so-called 'boomerang generation' of people in their 20s returning to live with their parents, but also, notably, family members moving in with younger relatives for companionship or care. [...]

One of the key incentives for lodging with another generation is financial. Those who moved in with others estimated that they save £225 per month on average, rising to £311 for young couples with no children. But for those providing the accommodation, the arrangement costs an average of £107 a month. [...]   (149 words)

Abridged from: *The Telegraph Online*, 22 August 2012

3

KATE MOSSE on the benefits of living with extended family

Three years ago, my husband and I bought an old house in the town we grew up in. […] It was just what we needed to house our two teenage children and my mother-in-law, who has been living with us since 1998. Plus, the self-contained ground floor
5 annexe meant my mother and father could join us. […] One address, two front doors, three generations. […]

My mother-in-law, in her late 70s now, is great company, funny, always playing the piano or knitting. Her living with us this past decade and more means our children have a proper
10 relationship with her. […]

The two households operate independently. My mother-in-law lives with us – so there are shared meal times, she does the ironing, I do the shopping, my husband the cooking and the admin – whereas my parents have their separate routines. […]

15 Of course, it wouldn't work for everyone – space, family history, finance, all sorts of reasons. But there are just as many reasons why it might. […]   (160 words)

Abridged from: *The Daily Mail Online*, 12 December 2009

4

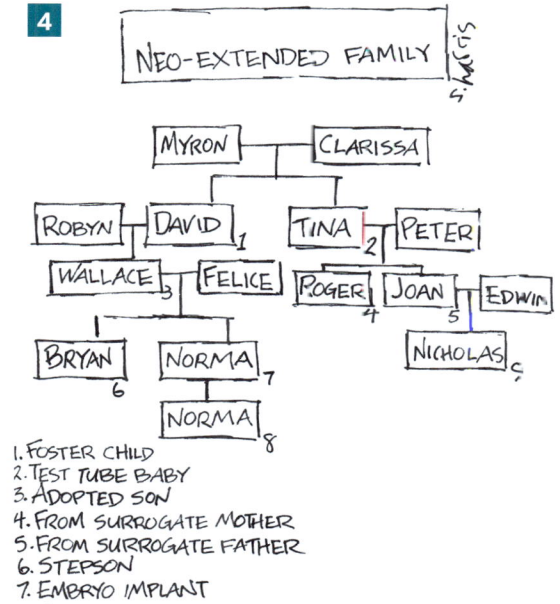

1. FOSTER CHILD
2. TEST TUBE BABY
3. ADOPTED SON
4. FROM SURROGATE MOTHER
5. FROM SURROGATE FATHER
6. STEPSON
7. EMBRYO IMPLANT
8. CLONE
9. NATURAL BIRTH

5

GENERATIONENGEMEINSCHAFT – ABER NICHT NUR ZUM EIGENEN VORTEIL

Was früher ganz normal war, könnte bald wieder im Trend liegen: die Großfamilie mit mehreren Generationen unter einem Dach. Eine solche „Wohngemeinschaft" bietet viele Vorteile für alle Beteiligten, allerdings sollten ein paar Grundregeln abgesteckt werden, bevor man das Projekt Großfamilie angeht. Denn die Erwartungen der einzelnen Parteien an die Mitbewohner können durchaus auseinander gehen.

5 Zunächst muss geklärt sein, ob es sich bei der Mehrgenerationen-WG um eine reine Zweckgemeinschaft handelt, oder ob sich die Beteiligten darüber hinaus ein gemeinsames Miteinander inklusive Austausch, Fürsorge und Verbundenheit wünschen. Beide Wege sind gangbar – nur muss über den Ansatz Einigkeit herrschen.

Darüber hinaus verspricht vor allem eine Konstellation Erfolg, in der keine der Generationen versucht,
10 die andere für ihre Zwecke einzuspannen, ohne sich selbst ebenso stark in die Gemeinschaft einzubringen. So sollten z. B. berufstätige Eltern die Großeltern nicht nur als ständig verfügbare (und preiswerte) Babysitter missbrauchen, und Senioren dürfen keine rundum Pflege erwarten, während sie sich z. B. um Kochen oder Hausarbeit drücken. Wichtig für die Gemeinschaft ist vor allem, dass sich keine der Generationen übervorteilt fühlt.

(171 words)

FURTHER OPTIONS

You are about to go and study in central London, but all the student accommodation is full. A friend has sent notes about a flat, but you want the student housing officer's advice.

Email the student housing officer (Mrs Winter) and ask what she thinks. Follow this email structure:

1 Remind Mrs Winter of yourself and your situation. Ask for her advice about the flat.
2 Give details of the place and the price.
3 Ask politely for Mrs Winter's opinion. Also ask if she has any better suggestions.
4 Say that you would be very grateful if she wrote back quickly because college starts next week.

> What about this place?
> 37 Park Rd, Morden , S London; 5-min walk shops & 7- min walk underground (+ about 1 hour college). 1-bed, 3rd-floor flat, part-furnished (kitchen white goods only). Single bedroom, kitchen-diner, bathroom. £1,250.00 pcm.

1 LISTENING

8

Eine Berufsberaterin vom britischen National Careers Service hilft einer Schülerin und einem Schüler bei der Wahl eines geeigneten Berufs. Hören Sie aufmerksam zu und vervollständigen Sie das Raster auf Deutsch und in Stichwörtern mit möglichst vielen Informationen aus dem Hörtext.

EXAM
→ Hörverstehen, SB S. 178

	Meera	Christopher
Alter	_____ 1	_____ 8
Traumjob	_____ 2	_____ 9
Freizeitaktivitäten	_____ 3	_____ 10
Lieblingsfach/fächer	_____ 4	_____ 11
Unbeliebteste(s) Fach/Fächer	_____ 5	_____ 12
Arbeitserfahrung/ Praktika	_____ 6	_____ 13
Empfehlung	_____ 7	_____ 14

2 LOOKING AT THE TEXT

→ Rezeption: Leseverstehen, SB S. 214

RETAIL JOB SEARCH FORUM
Europe's top recruitment agency

5

10

Employer:	Winter Adventure Centre
Location:	Muonio, Northern Finland
Job title:	Temporary waiter/waitress
Dates:	September – March
Working hours:	Minimum 40hrs per week incl. weekend work (Saturdays and Sundays), one month minimum
Pay:	€1,000 per month + tips + overtime
Benefits:	Free board and lodging in cottage in hotel complex Travel allowance of up to €300 for airfare to and from home country

Äkäskero is a small hotel and restaurant located 20km from the centre of the beautiful Pallas-Yllästunturi National Park, where husky safaris, snowmobiling, snowshoeing, ice fishing and cross-country skiing are popular winter activities.

15 We offer comfortable accommodation and a wide range of traditional Finnish and international cuisine and the successful candidate will be expected to wait on guests in the restaurant and assist elsewhere, as necessary. As there is no public transport, hotel vehicles can be used for leisure activities.

The successful candidate …

◊ is polite, friendly, helpful and flexible

◊ enjoys working with people of all ages and backgrounds

20 ◊ speaks good English and/or German

◊ has some experience as a waiter or is willing to learn

Have we described you? If so, send your application to Ms Laurukka Mäkelä, Director of Human Resources, through this website and we'll be in touch.

 UPLOAD CV  UPLOAD COVER LETTER

A Use the information in the advertisement to make notes on the following categories:

1 Length of contract _____

2 Allowance _____

3 Accommodation _____

4 Food _____

5 Insurance _____

6 Travel expenses _____

B Match the words in the box with the definitions below.

> waiter/waitress ▪ tip ▪ located ▪ range ▪ leisure ▪ experience ▪ willing ▪ application

1 CV and cover letter
2 free time
3 knowledge or skill gained from doing something
4 money given for good service, e.g. in a restaurant or hotel

5 person who serves guests in a restaurant
6 prepared or ready to do something
7 situated
8 variety

3 WORKING WITH WORDS

Use words from the box to complete the letter from a company director to his employees explaining why they now need to hot-desk. Two words will be left over.

> by default ▪ challenge ▪ downsize ▪ dress down ▪ filing cabinet ▪ gradual ▪ Human Resources ▪ property ▪ requires ▪ workforce

Dear colleagues,

I am sure you have all noticed the _____[1] changes that are happening around us. Five years ago we had a _____[2] of 350. Now the total number of employees is 575. In simple terms, our company is becoming too big for the building we are in.

So what can we do to deal with this _____[3]? One answer would be to _____[4] the company, but making it smaller would mean job losses. Another would be to look for a bigger building, but the price of _____[5] in our area is far too high.

Research has shown that not every employee _____[6] a desk every day, and some desks are even empty four days a week. We therefore intend to introduce hot-desking, which is when every employee has a _____[7] on wheels but no fixed desk. The new system will be demonstrated by the director of the _____[8] department next Monday at 10 am. We hope you will attend this very important meeting and look forward to your co-operation

Wallace Baxter
Managing Director

4 GETTING IT RIGHT

→ *If* sentences, SB S. 263

A Use the right form of the verbs in brackets (*if* sentences type 1) to complete the dialogue between a student and his mother.

Mother Have you seen this brochure about jobs, Nicholas? It says you _____[1] (not have) much chance of finding a good job if you _____[2] (not apply) early.

Student But not this early! If I _____[3] (send) an employer an application now, they _____[4] (tell) me to apply next year.

Mother But if you _____[5] (contact) them this year, they _____[6] (put) you on their waiting list, Nicholas! What's wrong with that?

Student It's stupid. If I _____[7] (change) my mind, I _____[8] (be) on the wrong waiting list.

Mother Well, I know from experience that you _____[9] (not find) anything if you _____[10] (wait) too long.

B Use the right form of the verbs in brackets (*if* sentences type 2) to complete the telephone conversation between Angela Jolly, a secretary at ICL computer services, and her friend Ramona, who is a school secretary.

Ramona Hi Angie! How are things?

Angela Could be better. I think I _____[1] (be) a lot happier if I _____[2] (have) a job like yours.

Ramona Well, if you _____[3] (work) here, you _____[4] (deal) with hundreds of people every week. Sometimes it's very stressful.

Angela Well, I'm at home alone all day working on the phone and the computer. It _____[5] (be) wonderful if I _____[6] (see) people every day! I think I _____[7] (accept) a pay cut if it _____[8] (mean) seeing more people again.

5 MEDIATION

Im Rahmen einer Projektwoche zum Thema Berufsfindung sollen Sie einen Beitrag für ein großes Plakat über die Situation von Jugendlichen in anderen EU-Ländern schreiben und finden folgenden Artikel über Großbritannien im Internet. Entnehmen Sie dem Text die relevanten Informationen über den Zusammenhang zwischen Berufsfindung und Jugendarbeitslosigkeit in Großbritannien aus Arbeitgeber- sowie Arbeitnehmer-perspektive. Beachten Sie auch die *Skills* Checkliste bevor und während Sie den Beitrag schreiben.

EXAM
→ Mediation, SB S. 179

SKILLS CHECKLIST: Written mediation

- ☑ Have I read the situation and instructions carefully?
- ☑ Have I read through the text and marked relevant information?
- ☑ Have I written the right sort of text?

Vocabulary notes

mismatch	*Missverhältnis, ungleiche Paarung*	gap	*Lücke*
sector	*Branche*	to reveal	*enthüllen, aufzeigen*
ratio	*Verhältnis*	locksmith	*Schlosser*
to commission	*in Auftrag geben*	surveyor	*(Land)vermesser(in), Gutachter(in)*
survey	*Studie, Umfrage*		

JOB *MISMATCH*

An employers' organization recently conducted a study among 11,000 teenagers currently at school in the UK. It found that over 25% of them were hoping for a job in the media, culture and sports *sector*, 18% wanted to be health professionals, but only 0.4% wanted a job in administration.

5   When the teenagers' ambitions were compared to the number of jobs actually on offer in the different sectors, it showed that 10 times more teenagers wanted jobs in the media, culture and sports sector than there were jobs available, so the *ratio* in this sector was 10:1. For health professionals the ratio was 3.5:1, but for administration the ratio was 1:20, meaning that there were 20 times more jobs available than teenagers interested in doing them. There were similar

10   ratios of 1:10 for hotels and restaurants and 1:6 for banking and finance.

    According to the employers' organization that *commissioned* the *survey*, there is a serious information *gap* between employers and teenagers. The result is that employers are in desperate need of suitable staff, whilst youth unemployment of 16- to 24-year-olds stands at over 14%, and many young people are looking for jobs that aren't available.

15   The survey also *revealed* that among the most popular jobs for young people were those of teacher, actor and police officer, whereas nobody wanted to be a *locksmith*, *surveyor* or speech therapist, all of which are well-paid jobs. One of the theories put forward to explain this phenomenon is that young people need role models to choose a job, but they only see them at school or in the media.

20   The report therefore suggests that employers should do far more to help young people find out about the various different jobs available. They should build up relationships with schools by visiting them and talking about their professions as well as offering work experience. The report also warns that information offered on websites or over the phone is no substitute for face-to-face advice given by qualified careers advisors.   (331 words)

Use vocabulary from the speech bubbles on page 74 of the student's book and the clues below to do the crossword.

Use vocabulary from the speech bubbles on page 74 of the student's book

FURTHER OPTIONS

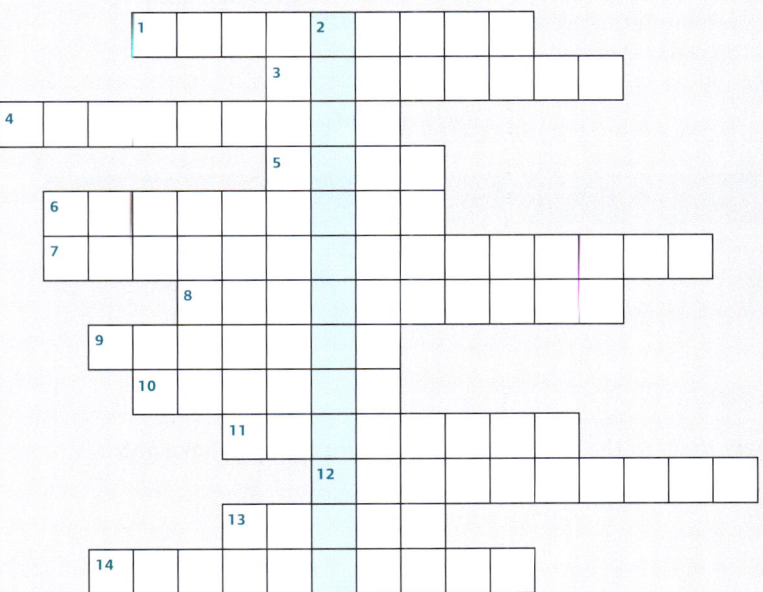

1 a building in which goods are stored
3 an arrangement whereby two people take it in turns to do the same job (3, 5)
4 a system in which employees can choose when they start and finish work
5 someone sent by an agency to do office work at a company for a short time
6 working regularly at different times of the day and night, e.g. one week from 6 am to 2 pm, the next week from 2 pm to 10 pm (5, 4)
7 the number of hours you spend per week working, compared with the number of hours you spend relaxing (4, 4, 7)
8 a long line of vehicles on a road that cannot move or can only move slowly (7, 3)

9 to record the time you arrive at work, e.g. by putting a card into a machine (5, 2)
10 a company or organization that arranges a service, e.g. travel, insurance, advertising
11 works, functions
12 a place where young children are looked after while their parents are at work (3, 7)
13 factory
14 paid work

1 BUILDING SKILLS

→ Gründliches Lesen, SB S. 223

A Read the questions and underline words that may help you to find the relevant areas of the text.

1 What sort of ethnic community did Benjamin Zephaniah grow up in?
2 What went wrong with his education?
3 What did the BBC poll show?
4 Why might we be surprised by this?
5 Why did he refuse the offer of the OBE?

SKILLS CHECKLIST:
Reading for understanding

☑ Have I looked for key words in the questions?
☑ Have I found the key words in the text?
☑ Have I compared my answers with the questions and the text?

B Read the text and underline key words that help to provide the answers.

BENJAMIN OBADIAH IQBAL ZEPHANIAH:

British poet, story-teller and song-writer

Born in Britain in 1958. His parents were both from the Caribbean islands, and he grew up in Handsworth, Birmingham – an area he calls 'the Jamaican capital of Europe'.
He left school at 13, unable to read or write. But with Jamaican music and poetry in his blood and angry street politics on his mind, he had a lot to say. He said it through public
5 performances of his hard-hitting poems. By the age of 15, he had *made a big name for himself* across Handsworth's large Jamaican and wider Afro-Caribbean community.

He did not fit well into the British social structure, and as a young man he was in trouble with the law and spent time in *prison*. Nor did his *anti-Establishment* ideas fit well, and over the years, he has continued his attacks on the Establishment. He has attacked, for
10 example, the British legal system, the monarchy, the political system, unfair treatment of minority groups in society and past *wrongdoings* of the British Empire.

Despite all this, he has also become one of Britain's most popular writers, and in a BBC poll he was voted the UK's third most-loved poet. He is Professor of Creative Writing at Brunel University, and his work is widely *recognized*.
15 However, he remains happily on the outside of society looking in. In 2003, for example, the Government offered him a medal, which he would receive from the Queen at Buckingham Palace. The medal was the OBE (short for The Order of the British Empire). His reply was immediate and clear though: 'Benjamin Zephaniah OBE – no way *Mr Blair*[1], no way Mrs Queen. I am *profoundly* anti-Empire.' (264 words)

[1] Tony Blair, Prime Minister from 1997 to 2007

Benjamin Zephaniah performing in London in 2010

Vocabulary notes

to make a name for yourself	*sich einen Namen machen*	wrongdoing	*Vergehen*
prison	*Gefängnis*	to recognize	*anerkennen*
anti-Establishment	*gegen das Establishment*	profoundly	*zutiefst*

C Write full answers to questions 1–5 in part A.

D Read your answers carefully and compare them to the questions to make sure that you have given the details required.

2 WORKING WITH WORDS

A Complete the table with words from the text in exercise 1.

Noun (person)	Noun (thing)	Noun (person)	Noun (thing)
performer	_____ 1	politician	_____ 3
poet	_____ / _____ 2	singer	_____ 4

B Use pairs of words from A to complete the following.

1 **A** Lucy is a good _____¹, and she plays the guitar well, too.

   B Yes, and did you know that she's recently started writing her own _____² as well.

2 **A** I don't like the way the _____³ are running this country!

   B Well, if you don't agree with them, you'll have to go into _____⁴ yourself and try to

   change things.

3 He is a great _____⁵, so the best way to experience his poetry is to go to one of his live

_____⁶.

4 Benjamin Zephaniah has written a number of stories such as *Refugee Boy*, but he first became known

as a _____⁷, and he is still most famous for his _____⁸, which are usually short,

often angry, and often funny, too.

→ *If sentences, SB S. 263*

3 GETTING IT RIGHT

Form type 3 conditionals from the following sentence parts, adding words as necessary. Start each sentence with *if*.

GETTING BACK TO AUSTRALIA

When Tom Blake was young, his family visited Australia on holiday. He loved the country and as he grew up, he often wished he could go back and get to know it better. Years later, with unemployment very high in the UK as he left college, his thoughts turned to Australia again.

1 unemployment not be so high in Britain / Tom find work without much difficulty

If unemployment had not been so high in Britain, Tom would have

_____

2 get job in UK / stay Britain quite happily

_____

3 things go well for him / not wonder about work in other countries

_____

4 never be to Australia / be certain never think about working somewhere so far away

_____

_____

5 not look for work there though / miss perfect job for him – as tour guide for visitors

_____

_____

6 not take tour group up Gold Coast / never meet perfect girl for him, and champion surfer
Jenny never become the love of his life!

_____

_____

4 **GETTING IT RIGHT**

→ Past perfect ■ Simple past, SB S. 255

Put the verbs in brackets into the simple past or past perfect.

After Alem's father (go) _____ ¹ back to East Africa, the authorities (give) _____ ²

the teenager a new life in England – just as his father (expect) _____ ³. Even though

Alem (never visit) _____ ⁴ England before, he soon (begin) _____ ⁵

to feel comfortable with his new family, school and friends. It (be) _____ ⁶ much more pleasant than

the dangers he (experience) _____ ⁷ at home in East Africa with his parents.

But then, one day, Alem (receive) _____ ⁸ a letter from his father with terrible news of

what (happen) _____ ⁹ to his mother. He (learn) _____ ¹⁰ that she

(disappear) _____ ¹¹ before his father's return from England. Then Alem (read)

_____ ¹² the thing that he (be) _____ ¹³ most afraid of: his father's letter

(explain) _____ ¹⁴ how he (finally find) _____ ¹⁵

her dead body near the border between Eritrea and Ethiopia.

5 **LISTENING**

9

**Sie hören ein Radiointerview über US Immigration von 1900 bis heute.
Lesen Sie zunächst die Sätze 1–12. Hören Sie dann aufmerksam zu und
vervollständigen Sie die Sätze auf Deutsch.**

EXAM
→ Hörverstehen,
SB S. 178

1   Im frühen 20. Jahrhundert sank die Anzahl der Immigranten zunächst. Dieser Trend setzte sich fort bis …
2   Zu diesem Zeitpunkt lag die Anzahl der Immigranten bei ungefähr 9,6 Millionen, bei einer
      Gesamtbevölkerung von knapp über …
3   Der Anteil der Immigranten an der Gesamtbevölkerung betrug demnach nur ca. …
4   Im Jahr 1980 lag der Anteil der Immigranten an der Gesamtbevölkerung bei ca. …
5   Die Gesamtbevölkerung der USA betrug zu diesem Zeitpunkt …
6   Um 1990 lag die Anzahl der Immigranten in den USA bei …
7   Damals lebten in den USA ca. 250 Millionen Menschen, also betrug die Zahl der Immigranten
      8 Prozent der …
8   Die Anzahl der Immigranten stieg dann auf 11 Prozent der Gesamtbevölkerung zu Beginn …
9   Zu diesem Zeitpunkt betrug die Anzahl der Immigranten in den USA …
10   Im Jahr 2012 betrug die Gesamtbevölkerung der USA …
11   Gleichzeitig gab es im Land …
12   Das sind ungefähr 13 Prozent der Gesamtbevölkerung der USA, und dieser Aufwärtstrend …

6 **BUILDING SKILLS**

→ Produktion: Statistiken beschreiben und analysieren, SB S. 238

Study the table to complete the analysis by circling the right words in brackets.

Population of the USA from 1870–1970 (millions)			
Year	Total	Immigrants	Percentage
1870	38.6	5.8	14.9
1890	63.0	9.7	15.4
1910	92.2	14.0	15.2
1930	123.2	14.4	11.7
1950	151.3	10.4	6.9
1970	203.2	9.6	4.8

SKILLS Checklist: Analysing figures

☑ Have I read the labels carefully?
☑ Have I understood the units that the
   figures are presented in?

Between 1870 and 1910, US immigrant numbers (rose / fell)¹ from (under / over)² six million to (a little under / almost exactly)³ fourteen million. At one point, their numbers (reached / fell to)⁴ 15.4% of the country's total population. However, from then until 1930, there was (little change / no change)⁵ in the immigrant population, while at the same time the total US population continued to (fall / increase)⁶ (rapidly / slowly)⁷ – from (around / exactly)⁸ 92 million in 1910 to (approximately / exactly)⁹ 123 million in 1930. This meant that as a percentage of the total, the trend was (downwards / upwards)¹⁰ – from 15.2% to just 11.7%. This (rise / fall)¹¹ continued until 1970, when immigrants formed (less than / more than)¹² 5% of America's population.

A Try to answer these questions based on the US citizenship test.

FURTHER OPTIONS

1 **Under the US Constitution, some powers belong to the states. What is one power of the states?**

   a to provide education ☐
   b to print money ☐
   c to create an army ☐
   d to make *treaties* ☐

2 **How old do *citizens* have to be to vote for President?**

   a twenty-one and older ☐
   b sixteen and older ☐
   c thirty-five and older ☐
   d eighteen and older ☐

3 **Who does a US Senator represent?**

   a Only the people in the state who voted for the Senator. ☐
   b The state legislatures. ☐
   c All state citizens in the Senator's political party. ☐
   d All citizens of the state. ☐

4 **What does freedom of religion mean?**

   a No one can *practise* a religion. ☐
   b You can practise any religion, or none. ☐
   c You can't choose when you practise your religion. ☐
   d You must choose a religion. ☐

5 **Name one branch or part of the US government.**

   a parliament ☐
   b the legislature ☐
   c the United Nations ☐
   d state governments ☐

6 **Who was President during the Great Depression and World War II?**

   a Herbert Hoover ☐
   b Calvin Coolidge ☐
   c Franklin D. Roosevelt ☐
   d Harry S. Truman ☐

7 **Name one state that borders Mexico.**

   a Arkansas ☐
   b California ☐
   c Florida ☐
   d Alabama ☐

Abridged and adapted from the *US Citizenship and Immigration Services' Naturalization Self-Test 1*

Vocabulary notes

treaty *Vertrag*   citizen *Bürger*   to practise *ausüben*

B Write two more questions (with a–d answers) that you think new US citizens should be able to answer. Try them out with a partner.

1 BUILDING SKILLS

→ Produktion: Schaubilder beschreiben und analysieren, SB S. 238

Foreign aid

In 1970 the world's richest countries promised to increase their annual aid budgets to 0.7% of gross national income (GNI). GNI means a country's income generated both inside and outside the country.

SKILLS CHECKLIST: Comparing figures in charts

☑ Have I pointed out the most striking features?
☑ Have I contrasted categories with each other?
☑ Have I described the relationships between the categories?

A Study the chart and say …

1 which country is closest to reaching the 0.7% target. _____

2 which country is furthest from the target. _____

3 which countries donate almost the same proportion of their GNI. _____

4 which English-speaking country donates the highest percentage of its GNI. _____

5 which country is in sixth place in the chart. _____

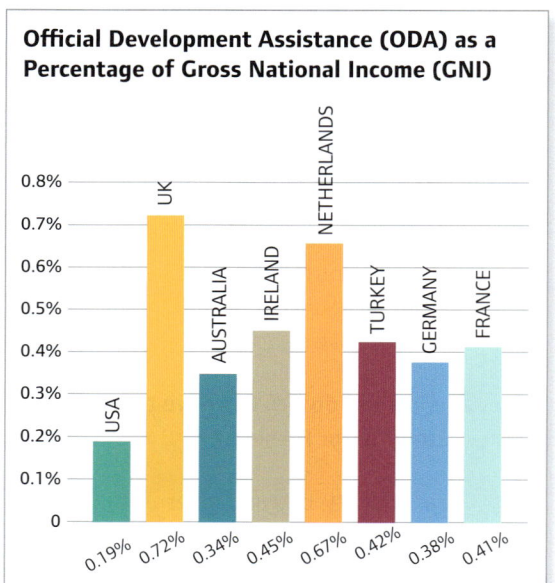

Official Development Assistance (ODA) as a Percentage of Gross National Income (GNI)

USA 0.19% | UK 0.72% | AUSTRALIA 0.34% | IRELAND 0.45% | NETHERLANDS 0.67% | TURKEY 0.42% | GERMANY 0.38% | FRANCE 0.41%

B Use expressions from the *Building skills* box on page 92 and the *Useful phrases* on page 93 of the student's book to complete the text.

The chart shows the _____ [1] of their GNI that rich countries spend on aid, and we can _____ [2] see that there are big differences. The UK is in first _____ [3] while Germany only _____ [4] sixth, and the figure in the first _____ [5] shows us that the USA is last. The _____ [6] for Germany (0.38%) is exactly _____ [7] as much as for the USA (0.19%). Australia (0.34%) spends about _____ [8] as much on aid as the Netherlands (0.67%).

C Study the chart about individual giving on page 92 of the student's book and compare it with this chart about government giving. Write 4–5 sentences to show the differences.

Begin like this: *Whereas private American individuals donate most money to help others, their government …*

2 LOOKING AT THE TEXTS

→ Rezeption: Leseverstehen, SB S. 214

A Read the texts on page 94 of the student's book and say if the following statements are true (T), false (F) or not in the text (N). Correct the false statements.

1 Kevin and Sandra Forkan were in Sri Lanka with four of their children. ☐

2 The children who survived were near the British Embassy. ☐

3 The British Embassy gave them a lot of help. ☐

4 The Forkan children were strong because their parents taught them to think of themselves first. ☐

5 The two brothers learned a lot about business when they travelled the world separately. ☐

6 They founded a flip-flop company in India with Mahatma Gandhi. ☐

7 The Gandys Foundation is a company which makes flip-flops. ☐

8 Paul and Rob Forkan plan to open more than one children's home. ☐

B **Can you find the words hidden in the anagrams below? The answers are all in the *Orphans for Orphans* text on page 94 of the student's book.**

1 LNBIGSSI ☐☐☐☐☐☐☐☐

2 EAIDCV ☐☐☐☐☐☐

3 TIHKHEIDCH ☐☐☐☐☐☐☐☐☐☐

4 ETTGNRHS ☐☐☐☐☐☐☐☐

5 RTAAIHINNMAU ☐☐☐☐☐☐☐☐☐☐☐☐

6 SEAPAOHRGN ☐☐☐☐☐☐☐☐☐☐

7 RLIVUVAS ☐☐☐☐☐☐☐☐

8 IYRCHAT ☐☐☐☐☐☐☐

3 **LISTENING**

🔊
10

In einem Podcast berichtet ein Reporter über die Arbeit der Stiftung *Rebuilding Sri Lanka*, die nach dem verheerenden Tsunami im Jahr 2004 gegründet wurde. Hören Sie aufmerksam zu und entscheiden Sie, ob die unten stehenden Aussagen über den Hörtext richtig (R) oder falsch (F) sind. Begründen Sie Ihre Entscheidung auf Deutsch.

EXAM
→ Hörverstehen, SB S. 178

Vocabulary notes

to borrow a book
ein Buch ausleihen

to lend a book
jdm. ein Buch leihen

1 The tsunami destroyed Clare Allen's hotel. ☐

2 After the tsunami, 40,000 Sri Lankans were homeless. ☐

3 The *Rebuilding Sri Lanka* charity has built five libraries. ☐

4 Schoolchildren who wish to pass their school-leaving exams receive £2,000 from the *Rebuilding Sri Lanka* charity. ☐

5 The *Rebuilding Sri Lanka* charity has a library which lends out more than 200 books every Saturday. ☐

6 The *Rebuilding Sri Lanka* charity provides schoolchildren with cheap meals at school. ☐

7 The *Rebuilding Sri Lanka* charity has a centre where counsellors can receive training. ☐

8 Most of the money donated to the *Rebuilding Sri Lanka* charity is spent on people in need. ☐

4 GETTING IT RIGHT

→ Present perfect ▪ Present perfect progressive, SB S. 252

A Write the present perfect forms of the verbs in the table.

Verb	Simple statement	Question	Negative
1 to ask (I)	I've ... ___ 1	Have I ... ___ 2	___ 3
2 to drive (you)	___ 4	___ 5	___ 6
3 to fall (she)	___ 7	___ 8	___ 9
4 to feel (we)	___ 10	___ 11	___ 12
5 to wear (they)	___ 13	___ 14	___ 15

B Now write the present perfect progressive forms of the same verbs in the table.

Verb	Simple statement	Question	Negative
1 to ask (I)	___ 1	___ 2	___ 3
2 to drive (you)	___ 4	___ 5	___ 6
3 to fall (she)	___ 7	___ 8	___ 9
4 to feel (we)	___ 10	___ 11	___ 12
5 to wear (they)	___ 13	___ 14	___ 15

C Complete the sentences with the present perfect or the present perfect progressive. Use the present perfect progressive when possible.

1 Rob and Paul Forkan _____ (write) a book called *Tsunami Kids*.

2 They _____ (sell) thousands of copies already.

3 The two brothers _____ (sell) Gandys flip-flops since 2012.

4 Katy Brown is a bookshop assistant and _____ (wear) her Gandys for eight hours, since she started work this morning.

5 She _____ (buy) two pairs of Gandys flip-flops.

6 So far this year Katy _____ (donate) £25 to charity.

7 Her shop _____ (start) to collect money for good causes.

8 She _____ (work) at the shop for two months now.

9 She _____ (serve) customers since 9 o'clock this morning.

10 Nine customers _____ (buy) a copy of *Tsunami Kids* today.

5 MEDIATION

EXAM
→ Mediation, SB S. 179

Ihrer Klasse nimmt am Schulprojekt „Umgang mit Minderheiten: Vielfalt und Integration" teil. Sie erhalten den Auftrag, einen Artikel für die Schülerzeitung über die Schwierigkeiten von Menschen, die an Autismus bzw. am Asperger-Syndrom leiden, zu schreiben. Darin sollen auch Integrationsinitiativen beschrieben werden. Sie finden folgenden Artikel in der Online-ausgabe einer amerikanischen Zeitung. Entnehmen Sie dem Text die relevanten Informationen und schreiben Sie Ihren Beitrag.

AUTICON

Anybody who has seen Dustin Hoffman in the 1988 Hollywood movie *Rain Man* will have an idea of what it means to *suffer from* autism. In the film, he plays a strange, *awkward* man living in his own world. However, he possesses *remarkable* mathematical skills and uses them to win large sums of money at the casinos in Las Vegas. In 2003, the novel *The Curious Incident of the Dog in the Night-Time*
5 described how someone suffering from only a mild form of autism, in this case Asperger's syndrome, can still find it hard to cope with the complexities of everyday life, but has no trouble at all with maths and physics and, in fact, anything that is logical and *predictable*.

Sadly, most autistic people are rejected for employment, so until recently, the future was *bleak* for anyone with this condition. But then businessman Dirk Müller-Remus from Berlin noticed that his
10 young son was able to copy US singer Usher's complicated dance steps on MTV *effortlessly*, however he had difficulty *relating to* his classmates and teachers at school. When Müller-Remus' musically-gifted son was diagnosed with Asperger's syndrome, his father spent a long time researching the illness. Müller-Remus realised that people with Asperger's had little chance of finding a job, so in 2011 he founded Auticon.

15 Auticon, with headquarters in Berlin, tests computer software and is the first company in Germany to exclusively employ software consultants suffering from Asperger's. They are able to use their exceptional mathematical abilities to *spot* errors in computer code and can do so quickly and reliably. Auticon has worked for big German companies such as Vodafone or Telekom, and it is an entirely self-supporting, profit-making enterprise. Auticon consultants receive training from job coaches who help
20 them understand the rules of *human behaviour*. But the main thing is that they can use their own very special skills to analyze software or company balance sheets. (317 words)

Vocabulary notes

to suffer from	*an etw. leiden*	effortlessly	*mühelos*
awkward	*unbeholfen*	to relate to sb/sth	*eine Beziehung [o. Zugang]*
remarkable	*bemerkenswert*		*zu jdm/etw finden*
predictable	*berechenbar, vorhersehbar*	to spot	*entdecken*
bleak	*düster*	human behaviour	*menschliches Verhalten*

FURTHER OPTIONS

Use the words in the box to complete the text. There are four more words than you need.

transplant ▪ science ▪ sign ▪ rushed ▪ willingness ▪ performed ▪ selflessness ▪ organ ▪ miracle ▪ medical ▪ kept ▪ donor ▪ discovered ▪ collapsed

While 62-year-old Peter Harris was in the garden, he suddenly felt ill and _____ [1].

Luckily, a neighbour saw it happen and called the emergency services. Peter was _____ [2]

to the local hospital in an ambulance and the doctors _____ [3] that he needed a

kidney _____ [4]. After six months, the hospital found a _____ [5]

and he received a new kidney. For Peter, getting his old life back again was like an act of God. He describes it

as a _____ [6]. Peter now regularly writes a blog called 'New Life', which has a link to the

_____ [7] donor register. He hopes that his readers will also _____ [8] up and save

lives. The first successful kidney transplant operation was _____ [9] in Illinois in 1950,

but since then the supply of kidneys has unfortunately not _____ [10] up with demand.

1 WORKING WITH WORDS

A Match these nouns from the text on page 100 of the student's book to the verb-noun pairs below.

action ▪ contact ▪ a contract ▪ an order ▪ quality

1 fill — a need / _____ / a position

2 lose — _____ / heart / sight of

3 make — a complaint / _____ / a mistake

4 raise — a price / _____ / a question/an issue/a matter

5 take — _____ / advice / place

B Replace the words in brackets with verb-noun pairs from part A. Make any changes necessary.

1 I think I've (got something wrong) _____ with these figures. They don't match the figures on the bill.

2 The Sunrise is a cheap, reliable car that (provides something necessary) _____ in the Indian market.

3 We've agreed that the next union meeting will (happen) _____ next Friday.

4 When Tony became unemployed, he tried hard to find a new job, but slowly he (stopped hoping) _____ .

5 Before the company decides to build the new factory, I'd like to (ask something) _____ _____ about costs.

6 I'm worried about this contract. Before we sign it, I think we should (ask somebody to advise us) _____ .

7 As western companies look for cheaper sources of supply in Asia, they often (forget) _____ that working conditions can be terrible in places like Bangladesh.

8 All our products are too cheap! We have to (increase the amount that we ask people to pay us) _____ , or we won't be able to stay in business for much longer!

2 GETTING IT RIGHT

→ The passive, SB S. 260

A Use the simple present passive to describe a process. Add 'by + agent' if necessary.

1 Farmers from all over the Gumutindo district grow coffee organically.

Coffee is _____

2 Then they bring the coffee to the new central production facility.

_____

3 There, highly-trained senior staff check quality and quantity.

_____

4 Then workers process the raw coffee in carefully-controlled conditions.

_____

5 After that, the Cooperative's new, automated equipment packs the coffee.

_____

6 Finally, they send the finished product to Mombasa for export to Europe and America.

_____

B **Turn Steve Race's spoken comments into part of a journalist's formal report. Put the underlined comments into the correct passive tenses. Add '_by_ + agent' if necessary.**

So it's finally happened – and I'm angry. The company owners up in New York have closed the factory here in Virginia, and they've thrown 200 workers out of our jobs. I hear they made the decision last summer, but they didn't tell the workforce till last month. It seems they'll send all the equipment from the Virginia plant to a new factory in Indonesia, and people there will produce the same furniture for a quarter of the pay.

But when they move production offshore like this, it exports American jobs, too, and that damages the American economy. Don't these New York money men understand? It's crazy! If we close every US factory, we will completely destroy the US economy. Then who will buy all those 'made in Asia' products?

200 JOBS LOST AT ACE FURNITURE
The ACE FURNITURE factory here in Virginia …

3 BUILDING SKILLS

→ Produktion: Cartoons beschreiben und analysieren, SB S. 236

Follow these steps to write a cartoon analysis:

1 Describe the cartoon.
2 Explain this ironic comment on the effects of globalization.
3 Use the newspaper headlines to explain further.
4 Comment on the manager's words in the cartoon.
5 Say what the cartoonist is attacking here.

Start like this: *This cartoon shows …*

> **SKILLS CHECKLIST: Describing cartoons**
>
> ☑ Have I read the caption(s) or speech bubble(s)?
> ☑ Have I described everything in the cartoon?
> ☑ Have I used the present progressive to describe what is happening?

DEVELOPED ECONOMIES NOT COMPETITIVE WITH FAR EAST

MANY US AND EUROPEAN JOBS EXPORTED TO DEVELOPING WORLD

UNCERTAIN FUTURE FOR WESTERN WORKERS

WE'RE GOING TO HAVE TO LET YOU GO…WE'VE FOUND SOMEONE IN CHINA WHO IS 45% BETTER AT BEING YOU FOR 24% LESS

4 LISTENING

EXAM
→ Hörverstehen,
SB S. 178

Sie hören eine Präsentation über die Kaffeeverkäufe der Gumutindo Cooperative.
Hören Sie aufmerksam zu und vervollständigen Sie dann die Sätze auf Deutsch.

1 Seit Gründung der Gumutindo Cooperative habe sich die Verkäufe positiv entwickelt – nach …

2 In der ersten Hälfte des ersten Jahres stiegen die Verkäufe schrittweise an, von null auf ca. …

3 Im zweiten Jahr wurde die Produktion auf bio umgestellt, was dazu führte, dass die Verkäufe für kurze Zeit …

4 Danach stiegen die Verkäufe des biologisch angebauten Kaffees schnell an und lagen bei 1.000kg im Monat …

5 Im dritten Jahr gab es ein stetiges Wachstum bei den Verkäufen, und am Ende der ersten Jahreshälfte lagen die Verkäufe bei …

6 Zur selben Zeit begann die Produktion von …

7 Dies wirkte sich auf die Verkäufe des unverarbeiteten Kaffees aus, und so gab es bis zum Ende des dritten Jahres nur …

8 Dieses Jahr haben die Verkäufe der Marke *Gold* …

9 Aus diesem Grund sanken die Verkäufe des unverarbeiteten Kaffees auf zunächst …

10 In der zweiten Jahreshälfte gab ein einen weiteren Rückgang auf …

5 TEXT PRODUCTION

EXAM
→ materialgestützter
Aufsatz, SB S. 180

'Globalization only ever benefits people and companies in rich countries.'

Write a composition. Use the information from at least three of the materials 1–4 and the cartoon on page 41.

1

It's a little known fact that Britain's largest manufacturer today is an Indian-owned conglomerate[1] called Tata. Over the past decade, Tata has taken over a series of famous British brands, from Jaguar, Land Rover and Tetley Tea to what's left of the once-mighty British Steel. Today Tata owns 19 European companies, in industries ranging from tea to IT, steel to cars, and employs 60,000 people in Britain.

5   Having invested more than £12bn in the British economy since 2000, Tata is fond of promising[2] that it will give back to the community far more than the profits it extracts. But the company is not immune to[3] global markets and slumping[4] commodities prices, and it has announced cuts in the UK in the past year affecting thousands of staff. [...]

Tata has long been India's biggest business, but Tata companies in the UK play down their Indian origins
10   and prefer to emphasise the Britishness of their brands. It's a strategy which has paid off remarkably well, especially at Jaguar, where an annual loss of £400m in 2008 turned almost overnight into handsome profits, big expansion and rapidly growing export markets, especially in China. Last November, the Queen opened Jaguar's new engine plant at Wolverhampton, in an acknowledgement of the private brand's success under its foreign owners.

Abridged from: *The Independent Online*, 05 February 2015

Annotations
[1] conglomerate – a large company formed by joining together different firms
[2] to be fond of promising sth – to say often that you will definitely do sth
[3] to be not immune to sth – to be open to being affected by sth
[4] slumping – (suddenly) falling

Negative Folgen für den Arbeitsmarkt

Sowohl in den Industrieländern als auch in den Entwicklungs- und Schwellenländern kann sich die globale Wirtschaftsweise negativ auf den Arbeitsmarkt auswirken, wenn auch in ganz unterschiedlicher Weise. Arbeitsplätze, die für wenig qualifizierte Arbeitnehmer geeignet sind, beispielsweise im Bereich der Warenproduktion, werden zunehmend in Billiglohnländer verlagert. Darunter leiden nicht nur die Industriestaaten, sondern auch die Arbeit-
5   nehmer in diesen Billiglohnländern, die nicht selten schlechte Arbeitsbedingungen wie unverhältnismäßig lange Arbeitszeiten und eine ungenügende soziale Absicherung hinnehmen müssen. Auch Kinderarbeit ist in diesen Ländern noch immer aktuell. Aus Sicht der Globalisierungsbefürworter sind jedoch sowohl der Arbeitsplatzmangel in Industrieländern, als auch die sinkenden Industrielöhne eher durch den technischen Fortschritt als durch Globalisierungsprozesse bedingt.

From: *www.globalisierung-fakten.de*

3

World Growth and Developing Country Growth
Annual % change in world real GDP and real GDP for developing countries

Source: *International Monetary Fund*

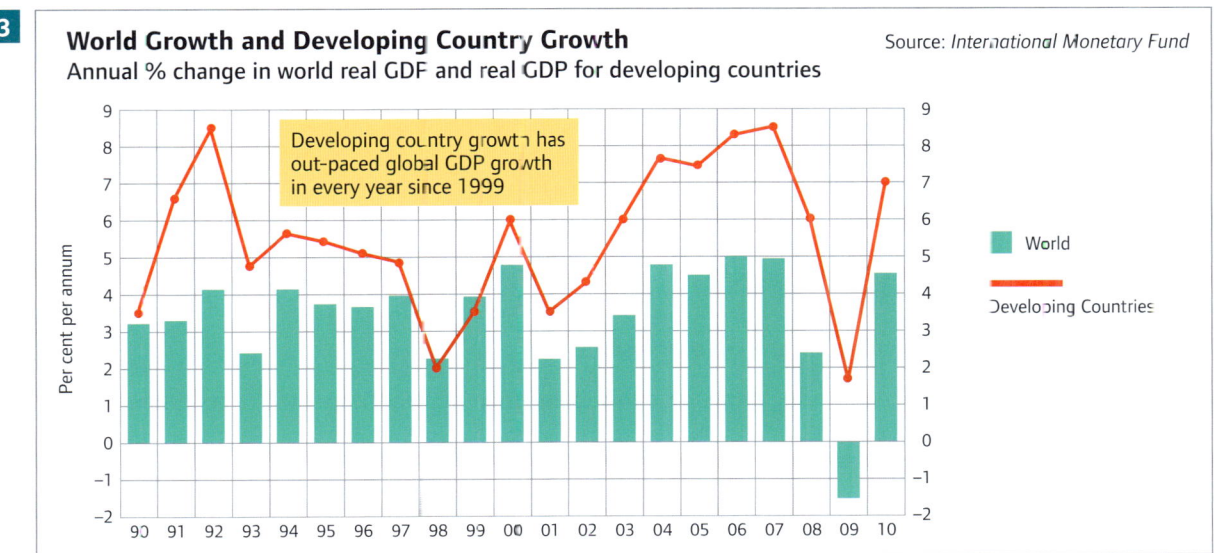

Developing country growth has out-paced global GDP growth in every year since 1999

■ World

— Developing Countries

4

'One of the great benefits of globalization is the manner in which it increases wage rates and purchasing power in previously low-income countries.'

Robert L. Thompson, Globalization and the benefits of trade

FURTHER OPTIONS

Read the role cards on page 177 of the student's book. Then match the sentences a–h below to the speakers on the right.

a The government has introduced expensive new legal requirements, including higher wages, so we need to put up our prices a little.

b Well, I know all about high transport costs, too – all the way to Europe. So I'm sorry, but I can't.

c If you pay me so little, how can I buy what I need to go on producing – or to feed my family?

d Sorry, but world prices are down, not up, so we need a price reduction or we'll have to import from South America instead of East Africa.

e Our costs are higher than ever, especially our insurance, due to all the pirate attacks east of Somalia. So I need to raise our prices.

f It's the best I can offer, and if you can't accept it, there are lots of other farmers who will.

g Sorry, but customers are looking for lower prices, so we're in a price war with our competitors. That means price reductions from our suppliers.

h You've got to give me a better price! I've got processing and storage costs and very high transport costs to send goods all over the country and then deliver them to you.

1 WORKING WITH WORDS

A Match words from box 1 with words from box 2 to form word pairs from the text on pages 110 and 111 of the student's book.

1

daytime • entry-level • job • middle • minimum • pay • production • retail • university • welfare

2

application • assistant • degree • industry • job • management • packet • system • TV • wage

B Use word pairs from A to complete the following sentences.

1 A lot of people don't earn enough to be able to support their families properly. The government needs to raise the _____ .

2 The _____ is very competitive. Look at the fierce competition between supermarkets, for example.

3 Tessa has always been interested in producing books and magazines, and now she's started work as a _____ with a big publisher.

4 Ralph was a junior manager for years, but now he has risen to a job in _____ .

5 Before the modern _____ was introduced, there was little to protect the poor, the elderly and the sick, apart from family, friends and charity.

6 I'm applying for an _____ job, so it isn't very well paid, but it's a good start.

7 Carla will have to study for another four years if she wants to get a _____ .

8 It's very hard to find work at the moment. I've sent out hundreds of _____ , but I've only been offered two interviews so far.

9 Tony isn't doing much about finding a job. He just sits at home and watches _____ .

10 I'm tired of being poor! I want to find a full-time job and get a proper _____ every month.

2 GETTING IT RIGHT

→ Modal verbs, SB S. 258

A Complete a reporter's interview with the publisher of the online publication *Business Now* by circling the right modal verbs in brackets.

Reporter	Is it true that you don't usually pay your contributors?
Publisher	That's right. In general, I find that we (needn't / mustn't)¹ pay because people want to give us their material anyway.
Reporter	But is that right? It seems to me that you really (should / might)² pay. I mean, how (might / can)³ writers go on writing if publishers don't pay them?
Publisher	Well, most people who write for *Business Now* (can't / don't have to)⁴ make money from it because they have other jobs.
Reporter	Yes, but your publication is a business like any other, and it seems to me that every business (must / may)⁵ pay its suppliers properly – or else it isn't a real business.
Publisher	No, no, you (needn't / shouldn't)⁶ think about it like that. You see, *Business Now* doesn't make big profits, so we simply (can't / mustn't)⁷ pay much. And remember this, we (have to / may)⁸ deal with many other costs, so free contributions help us to survive.

Reporter   So why do people do it?

Publisher   For various reasons, I think. For example, people (should / may) [9] write for *Business Now* because they want to share their ideas and help others in similar situations. There are others who (might / can't) [10] do it just to make a name for themselves in their own organizations.

B   Complete the dialogues. Use *can/can't* or *could/couldn't* when possible. When necessary, use forms of *(not) be able to*.

1   **A**   Have you prepared your new CV yet?

    B   I _____ [1] yet, but I _____ [2] have it ready by tomorrow.

2   **A**   How did you get on at your interview?

    B   Well, I _____ [1] see that they were quite interested in me, but I

    _____ [2] be sure that they were ready to offer me the job.

3   **A**   What about the general test that the company asks all candidates to do? A lot of people

    _____ [1] finish in the time that they allow.

    B   Yes, that went all right, I think, and I _____ [2] answer all the questions.

4   **A**   Well done for getting the job! But I hear that they wanted you to start on Monday, so why aren't you at work now?

    B   I _____ [1] start straight away because I had to go away. But I told them and

    luckily, I _____ [2] change the start date to next Monday.

3 LISTENING

A   Carlos, ein Student aus Brasilien, unterhält sich über Skype mit Peter North, der im Windsor Park Retirement Home wohnt. Hören Sie aufmerksam zu und vervollständigen Sie das Raster auf Deutsch mit Informationen aus dem Hörtext.

> **EXAM**
> → Hörverstehen, SB S. 178

Peter North	
Alter	1
Anzahl der Jahre im Altersheims	2
Gründe, weswegen er im Altersheim wohnt	3
Ehefrau	4
Familie (Kinder/Enkelkinder)	5
Alter der Enkelkinder	6
Ablauf der Woche / Hobbies	7
Peter Norths Meinung über das Altersheim	8

B   Hören Sie sich den Hörtext noch einmal an und entscheiden Sie, ob die folgenden Aussagen richtig (R) oder falsch (F) sind. Korrigieren Sie die falschen Sätze auf Deutsch.

1   This is the first time that Carlos has talked to this elderly American.   ☐

2   This person lived on his own for twelve years after his wife died.   ☐

3   He moved to Windsor Park Retirement Home because he was lonely.   ☐

4 His sons both have families, but not his daughter. ☐

5 His whole family gave him a surprise birthday party yesterday. ☐

6 They used the restaurant at Windsor Park. ☐

7 He enjoys various activities at Windsor Park, but he seems to enjoy going out even more. ☐

4 BUILDING SKILLS

→ Ein Wörterbuch benutzen, SB S. 217

Read the dictionary definitions (1–6) and match them to sentences a–f below.

work /wɜːk/ verb [I or T]   **1** to do a job, especially the job you do to make money   **2** If a machine works, it operates correctly.   **3** If you work a machine, you make it operate.   **4** to be effective, to go according to plan   **5** to arrange for something to happen, especially by doing it secretly and cleverly   **6** to shape, change or process a substance

a My computer isn't working properly: things keep disappearing from the screen. _____

b Cut the pastry into circles and then work them into little cups to hold the mixture. _____

c I'm only working part-time at the moment, so I'm looking for a full-time job. _____

d I worked it so that Tom and Ann sat together at dinner and had a chance to talk. _____

e It'll take three people for us to be able to work this old machine properly. _____

f The medicine started to work almost immediately, and Sam soon began to feel better. _____

5 MEDIATION

EXAM
→ Mediation, SB S. 179

In Ihrer Jugendgruppe ist die alternde Gesellschaft derzeit Thema. Nächste Woche geht es um die Frage: „Wie kann man dem demographischen Wandel in Deutschland begegnen?" Sie beschließen, über Mehrgenerationenhäuser zu recherchieren und finden folgenden Artikel im Internet. Entnehmen Sie dem Text die relevanten Informationen und schreiben Sie eine Zusammenfassung für die Website Ihrer Gruppe.

With the number of over-65s set to double [...], *Mehrgenerationenhäuser* may be the answer

In Pattensen, a small town of 13,000 just south of Hanover, pensioners play cards to the echoing tick-tock of a grandfather clock. It might be a melancholy scene – if it wasn't for the squeals of delight coming through the open door from the nursery on the next floor.

5 The nursery and the sitting room are part of a *Mehrgenerationenhaus*, literally a 'multigeneration house', which is a kindergarten, a social centre for the elderly and somewhere young families can drop in for coffee and advice. In theory, the sitting room is reserved for the over-60s, but in practice the door to the kids' area rarely stays closed for long.

Pensioners volunteer to read books to the children once a week and run a 'rent-a-granny' service to relieve exhausted parents. In return, teenagers offer to show elderly people how to use computers and mobile phones.
10 Maria Mantei, 66, and her husband Lothar, 71, who is blind, joined the centre two years ago after the death of their daughter. 'We had hit rock-bottom, but we didn't want therapy, we just wanted to be among people again,' she said.

Every Monday morning, when people with dementia use the sitting room for games and singing, children join in without being prompted. 'Kids are more at ease dealing with dementia patients than adults,' said Angela
15 Schulz, one of the care workers leading the sessions, 'so we find patients are much more relaxed here than anywhere else.'

Britain, too, may soon start to send its pensioners to nurseries or babies to nursing homes. Last week, a report by the Institute for Public Policy Research urged Britain to adopt the *Mehrgenerationenhaus* approach to cope with an ageing population. The number of over-65s in Britain is expected to almost double by 2030, and childcare
20 in Britain is more expensive than almost anywhere in the world. Could both problems be tackled in one swoop?

'Multigenerational houses are a key part of Germany's ageing population plan,' said the report [...]. 'In the years ahead, these approaches will not be a "nice to have" but a necessity, as families will need an extra helping hand to cope with caring responsibilities and pressure grows to contain the rising public costs of health and social care.' [...]

25   But if the big idea behind Germany's multigenerational houses is to see demographic change as an opportunity not crisis, one criticism is that they have not actually risen to the size of the challenge: a recent government report predicted that by 2060 every third German would be aged 65 or over.

Student-style housing blocks for pensioners are increasingly popular in Germany, and some of them, like the Amaryllis centre in Bonn, actively try to keep a balance of young families and the elderly. A recent report suggested

30   co-habitation could reduce the cost of care for the over-50s by 30–50% per head. Yet until now such projects have been largely run as co-operatives, with no serious support from the state.

'Co-habitation projects could be the future for ageing countries in Europe,' said Andrea Tøllner, who advises local governments on the creation of new housing projects. 'But the key is to remind people they can always close their door if they want. They're not going back to student flatshares but separate living units.'

35   The pensioners at Pattensen came to that realisation long ago. Between 2:30 and 5 every Thursday afternoon, the door to the sitting room remains shut so they can play cards in peace.   (574 words)

Abridged from: *The Guardian Online*, 2 May 2014

**FURTHER
OPTIONS**

Read the notes about members of the Carter family. Use the notes
a) to complete a paragraph about Mark and
b) to continue paragraphs about Jack and Will.

Mark Carter 2000 – (?) 2080/90	**Jack Carter 1900 – 1970**	**Will Carter 1800 – 1850**
Family: parents, 1 sister **Home:** 3-bedroom house just outside Birmingham **Education:** 2 years at nursery school; 13 years at state school; (?) 3–4 years at university **Employment:** many options, (?) software designer **Travel:** farthest so far: Florida, USA; by plane	**Family:** parents, 6 brothers and sisters **Home:** small terraced house in central Birmingham **Education:** 8 years at state school; 2 years of night classes at technical college **Employment:** car mechanic **Travel:** farthest ever: London; by train	**Family:** parents, 11 brothers and sisters **Home:** small farm cottage in a village ten miles from Birmingham **Education:** 1 year at the village church school **Employment:** Farm worker **Travel:** farthest ever: the new industrial town of Birmingham; on foot

Social changes across seven generations of the Carter family

Mark Carter was born in _____ , and he will probably live to the age of _____ or _____ .

He lives with his _____ in _____

_____ . He is growing up with a normal early

21st-century education of _____ and _____

_____ , and probably also _____ .

As for employment, he will have _____ , but he may become _____

_____ . The farthest that he has travelled so far is to _____ ,

and he went there _____ .

Mark's life is very different from that of his great-grandfather Jack. Jack Carter was born in ... , and he died in ...

Mark's life is even more different from that of great-grandfather Jack's own great-grandfather Will. Will Carter was ...

1 LOOKING AT THE TEXT

→ Grobverständnis, SB S. 214

A Skim the text quickly and decide which statement best describes what it is about.

a Young Muslim girls from poor families are running away to the Middle East.

b Young Muslim girls who run away feel that Western society doesn't value them.

c Recent migrants are more in favour of terrorism.

UK MUSLIM COMMUNITY
DEVASTATED BY RUNAWAY JIHADI BRIDES

The press regularly write stories about young European men leaving to become foreign fighters in the Middle East and returning to Europe as hardened terrorists, but it took a little longer
5 for society to realize that young girls were also leaving and rarely coming back. The UK's Muslim community is so *devastated* that in September 2014, Muslim women launched the 'Making A Stand' campaign to stop their children, in particular
10 their daughters, running away and joining extremist groups in the Middle East.

In a moving letter to all young Muslim girls thinking of going out to join ISIS, they remind them that in the ISIS *caliphate*, girls should marry
15 from the age of nine and women wear *veils* and are kept out of sight of society. They tell them that once in Syria or Iraq they will not be allowed to leave the caliphate and return to the UK, adding that many have tried but few have succeeded.
20 They warn the young Muslim girls that they will have no chance to fulfil any dreams they may have about a better life and will lose their identity and freedom, because ISIS treats women as second-class citizens and not with the *dignity* and respect they
25 are promised in Islam.

So what makes a young person decide to run away? A University of London study found that young Muslims *sympathizing* with terrorism were often born and brought up in the UK, had enough money but were socially isolated and suffered from
30 depression. Recent migrants to the UK who came to the West to escape violence and war were found to be less ready to support radical ideas.

Another study found that Western society does not give young Muslims the feeling that they belong.
35 Instead, they feel that society does not value them and in some cases places *restrictions* on how they can *practise* Islam, e.g. the burqa ban in France and Belgium. It describes how the leader of ISIS offers young women a new life in which they can help
40 create a pure Islamic state with a variety of jobs and responsibilities for women, such as being a member of an all-women moral police force which makes sure that other women *keep* strictly *to* ISIS's interpretation of Sharia law. The study finishes by
45 saying that the young women's reasons for joining the jihadis in the Middle East are not only political but also personal, with a strong element of naive romanticism.

(408 words)

Vocabulary notes

devastated	*am Boden zerstört*	to sympathize	*sympathisieren*
caliphate	*Kalifat*	restriction	*Einschränkung*
veil	*Schleier*	to practise	*ausüben*
dignity	*Würde*	to keep to	*einhalten*

B Answer the questions about the text in exercise 1 in your own words as far as possible.

→ Umgang mit Operatoren, SB S. 232

1 Outline the problem that has shocked the UK's Muslim community.

2 Describe the action taken by the Muslim community to counteract this problem.

3 Contrast the life that a young Western woman can expect in the ISIS caliphate as described by its leader and by the members of *Making A Stand*.

4 Examine the factors which may make a young woman decide to become a jihadi bride.

2 MEDIATION

EXAM
→ Mediation, SB S. 179

Nachdem mehrere junge Deutsche – auch Frauen – nach Syrien ausgewandert sind, um sich extremistischen Gruppen anzuschließen, regt die Lokalzeitung eine öffentliche Diskussion über die Beweggründe der jungen Menschen hierfür an. Im Internet finden Sie den Artikel über die Reaktion britischer Musliminnen, als klar wurde, dass mehrere muslimische Schülerinnen aus London weggelaufen waren, um im sogenannten ISIS-Kalifat Dschihadisten zu heiraten (siehe Übung 1). Schreiben Sie einen Leserbrief an die Zeitung, in dem Sie schildern, was für ein Leben die jungen Frauen im Kalifat erwartet, und was sie evtl. dazu bewogen hat, ihr Leben im Westen aufzugeben.

3 WORKING WITH WORDS

A Complete the word families using forms from the text in exercise 1.

Verb	Noun	Noun (person)	Adjective
to terrorize	terrorism	_____	
to _____ 2	reminder		
to _____ 3	success		successful
to _____ 4	fulfilment		fulfilling
to free	_____ 5		free
to _____ 6	treatment		treatable
to dignify	_____ 7		dignified
to _____ 8	promise		promising
to migrate	migration	_____ 9	migratory
_____	_____ 10		violent
to restrict	_____ 11		restrictive
to _____ 12	practice		

B Use ten of your answers in A to complete the text below. Make any necessary changes.

It is all too easy to see the young women who run away to _____ [1] their dreams in Iraq or Syria as dangerous _____ [2] just like the armed Islamic fundamentalists we often see on TV. It may seem strange but, just like other teenagers, they are simply rebelling and looking for their _____ [3]. They find that the _____ [4] placed on Islam by Western society (e.g. the burqa ban) make it impossible for them to _____ [5] their religion in the way they wish. They expect to be treated with _____ [6], but the mass media's Islamophobia _____ [7] them every day that they do not belong. Some young Muslim girls actually _____ [8] in reaching the caliphate and arrive expecting that the people there will _____ [9] them with respect. Many are then shocked by the extreme _____ [10] of the ISIS fighters, but by then it is too late to leave.

4 LISTENING

EXAM
→ Hörverstehen,
SB S. 178

In einer Talkshow im Radio diskutieren die Teilnehmer die Vor- und Nachteile von Überwachungskameras. Lesen Sie sich zunächst die Sätze 1–6 kurz durch. Hören Sie dann aufmerksam zu und vervollständigen Sie die Sätze auf Deutsch.

1 Der Polizist ist grundsätzlich für den Einsatz von Überwachungskameras, weil …

2 Die Journalistin räumt ein, dass Kameras nützlich sein können, glaubt aber, dass …

3 Laut Aussage des Schauspielers müssen zwei wichtige Faktoren bei der Aufstellung von Überwachungskameras berücksichtigt werden, und zwar …

4 Die Aussage der Studentensprecherin ärgert den Polizisten, weil …

5 Die Studentensprecherin zweifelt an der schützenden Rolle der Polizei, weil …

6 Die Journalistin meint, dass der Schauspieler sich widerspricht, weil …

5 GETTING IT RIGHT

→ Verb + infinitive ▪ Verb + gerund, SB S. 261

Choose an infinitive or gerund to complete these sentences. Sometimes there are two possible answers.

Digital dilemma

Banks encourage us (to open / opening)[1] an online account, shops want us (to download / downloading)[2] their app and more and more people are choosing (to shop / shopping)[3] online rather than in a crowded department store – but there's a downside. Opening any kind of digital account involves (to give / giving)[4] personal information to an organisation. Some people don't mind (to do / doing)[5] this and don't hesitate (to provide / providing)[6] their bank account and credit card details. Experts therefore recommend (to use / using)[7] a different, strong password for each of our accounts and some even suggest (to change / changing)[8] these passwords every few months. This is where the digital dilemma begins. At first sight, a modern digital lifestyle seems (to be / being)[9] fast and convenient, and we like (to have / having)[10] more time for leisure activities. However, we can't afford (to lose / losing)[11] all our money to data thieves, so we constantly need to change our passwords. One way to avoid (to have / having)[12] all this stress is to buy things in shops again and use paper for our bank transactions.

6 BUILDING SKILLS

→ Interaktion, SB S. 246

Use the expressions in the box to fill in the gaps in the discussion. You can look at the *Useful language* on the back flap of the student's book if you need help.

> Do you see what I mean? ▪ I couldn't agree more! ▪ I see what you mean ▪
> I'm afraid I can't accept ▪ I'm sorry to interrupt, but ▪ If you ask me ▪ Let me put it in another way ▪
> So, is the basic idea that ▪ The main reason is ▪ There's some truth in what you say ▪
> Well, as a matter of fact ▪ What's your view on

Listeners are phoning in to speak on the BBC radio talk show *World have your say*. The topic for discussion is surveillance cameras.

Talk show host   … Just stay on the line for a moment will you, Ronald? Let's hear what our next caller thinks. It's Margaret in Ireland. Why do you think we need more surveillance cameras, Margaret?

Margaret   _____[1], people are more out of control these days, especially young people, so we need cameras in schools as well.

Talk show host   And why are they out of control, Margaret?

Margaret   _____[2] that school doesn't give them enough to do, so they do stupid things in their free time.

Talk show host _____ [3] surveillance cameras in schools, Ronald? Is it a place where young people have too much free time and are out of control?

Ronald _____ [4]! Margaret's exactly right! We should have cameras in schools.

Talk show host We should have surveillance cameras in schools, say Margaret and Ronald. Our next caller is Noureddine in Morocco. Do you agree with Margaret and Ronald?

Noureddine _____ [5], I don't. Schools are a place of learning where people must feel free. They shouldn't be a place where 'Big Brother is watching you', so _____ [6] the idea that we need to keep control of young people with surveillance cameras.

Talk show host So what do you say to Noureddine about that, Margaret?

Margaret _____ [7] because young people need _some_ freedom. A school shouldn't be like a prison, so _____

_____ [8]. But I do believe there isn't enough discipline. _____

_____ [9]: Imagine if you sent your child to your local school and found out they were doing drugs at lunchtime. You'd be really worried wouldn't you? So _____ [10]? You think your children are learning what they need for life and all they're doing is learning to break the law!

Talk show host _____ [11] if you give young people too much freedom, they'll break the law, Margaret? If you really believe that …

Noureddine _____ [12] I think that what Margaret is suggesting is completely wrong …

A **Match words in box 1 with words in box 2 to form collocations from the three texts on page 134 of the student's book.**

FURTHER OPTIONS

1
classified ■ death ■ diplomatic ■ geographical ■ global ■ household ■ mass ■ natural ■ recent ■ uncontrolled ■ volcanic ■ warning

2
area ■ cables ■ disasters ■ epidemic ■ eruptions ■ material ■ name ■ outbreak ■ proportions ■ surveillance ■ systems ■ toll

B **Use six of your answers in A to complete the text.**

_____ [1] sent by the US and UK embassy staff to their governments in response to the Ebola crisis made it clear that the _____ [2] could easily spread over a large _____ [3] if the world did not act quickly. In the case of _____ [4] like earthquakes or hurricanes, the media rush to the location to get dramatic pictures, but when there is an _____ [5] of a killer disease, this tends to be under-reported. The _____ [6] can therefore only be estimated, and in the case of Ebola it varies between 9,000 and 14,000 fatalities.

1 WORKING WITH WORDS

Each of the first sentences contains a word from pages 136 and 137 of the student's book in *italics*. Complete the second sentences with a word with a similar meaning from the box. Make any necessary changes.

> appear ▪ grow ▪ hugely ▪ lift ▪ opportunity ▪ reason for ▪ stop

1 Developing countries all aim to *raise* their levels of economic activity. By doing this, they can _____ their people out of poverty.

2 With China's rapid rise as a great economic power, its industries have developed *massively*. As we would expect, the country's energy needs have also increased _____ .

3 What's the *cause* of the increasing levels of CO_2 in the atmosphere? Most climate scientists agree that human activity is the main _____ this worrying change.

4 What happens if we can't *prevent* CO_2 levels from reaching 560ppm? If we don't _____ that from happening, most scientists say that disastrous climate changes will follow.

5 It's hard to be sure, but climate change *seems* to be happening already. For example, we _____ to get more wet weather in winter than we used to.

6 During the heaviest rains that have ever been recorded, the rivers *expanded* to twice their normal size last year. And the lakes _____ to three times their usual area.

7 The next international meeting on climate change offers another *chance* to control global CO_2 emissions. And that will give the world another _____ to limit climate change.

2 GETTING IT RIGHT

→ Indirect speech, SB S. 265

A **Report part of a debate on climate change. Use full forms of the reporting verbs in the simple past. (Some are in brackets, others are underlined.)**

Sally Miller:
(state) Climate change is nothing new because it's happening all the time: it always has done, and it always will. So I <u>don't think</u> that the Greens can blame humans for something that's just part of nature.

Mark Farina:
I <u>don't agree</u>. (point out) There's a clear connection between the rise in CO_2 levels that began with the Industrial Revolution and the warming that the world has seen since then. (go on to say) The more CO_2 people throw into the atmosphere, the more temperatures will continue to rise.

B **Rewrite the questions as indirect questions, using the reporting verbs in brackets. (The reporting verbs should be in the simple past.) Make any other changes that are necessary.**

Back in London after the Brussels trip, Julie's friends had lots of questions.

1 **Kate:** 'Does your newspaper often send you on jobs like that?' (ask)

   Kate asked if her newspaper often _____

2 **Chris:** 'How long were you away?' (want to know)

   _____

3   Lisa: 'Did you interview anyone interesting?' (wonder)

_____

4   Ellie: 'What did you talk to Matt Radley about?' (inquire)

_____

5   Tom: 'Did he answer your questions properly?' (ask)

_____

6   Jean: 'Have you written your report yet?' (inquire)

_____

7   Tom: 'When can we read it in the paper?' (want to know)

_____

8   Ben: 'Where do you think they'll send you next?' (wonder)

_____

C   Rewrite the requests, instructions and advice in indirect speech, using the reporting verbs in brackets. Make any other changes that are necessary.

The Brussels trip had been Julie's first big job, so her editor Tony Good wanted a meeting about it. He called Julie and said, 'Come to my office for a chat as soon as you're free.' (tell … to) 'Could you give me a bit longer so that I can finish my report?' Julie replied. (ask … to) So Tony gave her a time, and he also said, 'Email me the report before you come to let me have a quick look at it.' (requested .. to) Julie agreed, and then she said, 'Perhaps you could suggest ways I can improve it.' (ask … to)

The Brussels trip had been Julie's first big job, so her editor Tony Good wanted a meeting about it. He

called Julie and told her to come to his _____

Julie asked _____

So Tony gave her a time, and he also _____

_____

_____

Before the meeting, Tony contacted the Features Editor, Tania Ray, and asked, 'Would you like to come to my office to discuss Julie Branson's report?' (invite … to) Both the editors liked the report, but Tony said to Julie, 'I think you should reduce it by about 100 words so that we can include a visual.' (advise … to) Then he called Alan Carter in the Art Department and said, 'I want you to prepare a visual that will show the fracking process.' (instruct … to) Finally, at the end of the meeting, Julie made a big request. She said, 'Tony, could you send me to find out how local people feel about the fracking project? Please!' (beg … to)

Before the meeting, Tony contacted the Features Editor, Tania Ray, and _____

_____

Both the editors liked the report, but Tony _____

_____

_____

_____

_____

_____

3 LISTENING

14

Julie hat einige Leute gefragt, was sie über das Fracking-Projekt denken. Hören Sie aufmerksam zu und beantworten Sie anschließend die unten stehenden Fragen auf Deutsch in ganzen Sätzen.

EXAM
→ Hörverstehen, SB S. 178

1 Warum findet Jenny Wade es verrückt, noch mehr fossile Brennstoffe aus der Erde zu holen?
2 Was sollte man ihrer Meinung nach stattdessen tun?
3 Worüber ist Stella King beunruhigt?
4 Über wen macht Stella sich besondere Sorgen?
5 Warum ist Lyn Benson für das Projekt?

6 Wie denkt Brian Fox über erneuerbare Energien?
7 Was spricht Brians Meinung nach für die Nutzung von Gas?
8 Wer wird, laut Alan Smith, von diesem Projekt profitieren, und wer wird darunter leiden?
9 Wie beschreibt Bob Lowe die Entwicklung des Projekts?
10 Wie könnte Bob davon profitieren?

4 TEXT PRODUCTION

'How can we feed the growing demand for energy worldwide – without destroying the planet?'

EXAM
→ materialgestützter Aufsatz, SB S. 180

Write a composition. Use the information from at least three of the given materials.

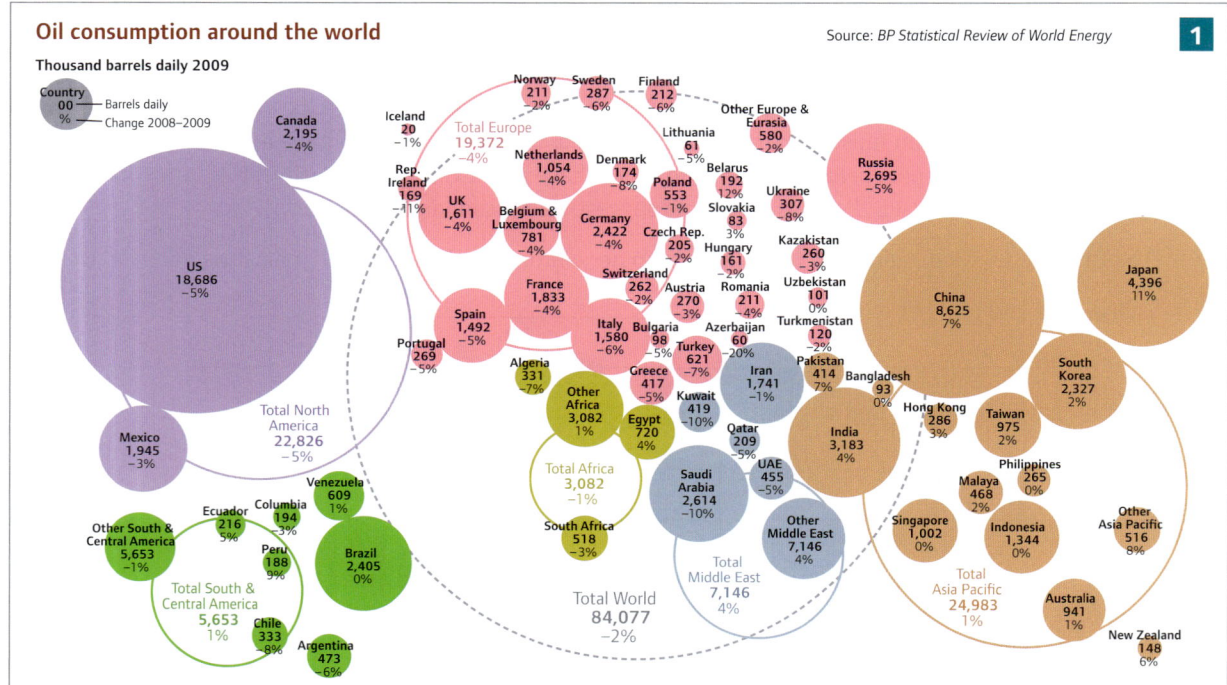

Oil consumption around the world
Source: *BP Statistical Review of World Energy* 1

UN-Dekade 2

Nachhaltige Energie für alle
Die 193 Mitgliedsstaaten der Vereinten Nationen (UN) haben [...] 2013 in New York einstimmig die Jahre 2014 bis 2024 zur „Dekade der nachhaltigen Energie für alle" erklärt. Ziel ist es, nahezu allen Menschen Zugang zu Ener-
5 gieversorgung zu ermöglichen. Um zugleich den Klimawandel zu stoppen, muss die Energie nachhaltig und umweltfreundlich erzeugt werden.

Hauptziele bis 2030
Zugang zu Strom und moderne Energieformen für alle Menschen weltweit. Nachhaltige Entwicklung ist nicht möglich ohne nachhaltige Energie. Energie
10 unterstützt die soziale und wirtschaftliche Entwicklung und bietet Gelegenheit für eine verbessertes Leben und wirtschaftlichen Fortschritt. Deshalb sei ein universeller Zugang zu modernen Energien unbedingt notwendig, um die Millenniums-Entwicklungsziele zu erreichen. [...]   (109 words)
Abridged from: *www.bundesregierung.de*, 01 April 2014

'If history is any guide, oil will eventually be overtaken by less-costly alternatives well before conventional oil reserves run out. Indeed, oil displaced coal despite still vast untapped reserves of coal, and coal displaced wood without denuding our forest lands.'
Alan Greenspan
(US economist, Chairman of the Federal Reserve of the United States from 1987–2006)
 3

4

WHAT WAS THAT THUD?

THE WEST

DEVELOPING WORLD'S CARBON FOOT PRINTS

DEVELOPED WORLD'S CARBON TYRE TRACKS

CHRIS MADDEN

Demand for energy is growing: What can we do to provide enough for everyone safely and efficiently?

Providing enough energy for the world is becoming a problem. We struggle to do it now, with 20 per cent of the world's population (1.3 billion people) already living without electricity, and by 2050, there will be another 2 billion people living on this planet. And as the world's dependence on technology grows, the amount of energy we will need in the future could be more than we now expect. The International Energy Agency estimates that we will need $38 trillion to pay for all the energy the world will require between now and 2035. Of that demand, 90 per cent will come from developing countries and economies.

An added problem is the change from traditional sources of energy like fossil fuels and nuclear power to cleaner, greener energy sources. The change is necessary for the environment but difficult, as many countries still rely on the traditional sources. Despite this, over half of our energy comes from renewable sources today, and experts are positive that an increase is possible. The International Panel on Climate Change estimates that by 2050, 77 per cent of energy demands could be met by renewable sources. As the prices for these sources, e.g. geothermal energy, wind and solar power, are falling, they are also becoming more cost-effective, especially when you consider the full cost of using fossil fuels (including mining, transportation etc.).

(227 words)

5

10

15

5

FURTHER OPTIONS

A Read the following energy-saving suggestions for a new town. Decide which would be:

* reasonably cheap   * quite expensive   * very expensive

Ways of saving energy			
1 Provide free out-of-town car parks to reduce city-centre traffic.			
2 Provide low-cost bus transport to and from the car parks.			
3 Provide free bus transport to and from the car parks.			
4 Provide free public transport for everyone across the city.			
5 Check and charge all private vehicles for entering the city.			
6 Provide free bicycles for all to use across the city.			
7 Provide all-weather clear-plastic tunnels for cyclists across the city.			
8 Stop all public transport at 11 pm.			
9 Turn off all street lights at 11 pm.			
10 Reduce heating in all public buildings, e.g. council offices, schools & libraries.			
11 Provide 50% subsidies to help people make their homes energy efficient.			

B You are a candidate for the new town council. Write two paragraphs. In paragraph 1 support two suggestions, in paragraph 2 reject two suggestions. Follow this structure:

		happy			support			the idea of …ing	
I am (also)				to say that I					
		sorry			do not support				

	think		offer	limited			high	
I	believe	it would	produce	useful	benefits	at a (very)		cost.
	am sure		create	major			reasonable	

1 WORKING WITH WORDS

A Add vowels (a, e, i, o, u) to form two-word expressions from page 147 of the student's book.

1 grnhs gss _____

2 clmt chng _____

3 nvrnmntl plltn _____

4 glbl wrmng _____

5 ntrl rsrcs _____

6 crbn mssns _____

B Use expressions from A to complete the following text.

When the Industrial Revolution began using _____

_____[1] such as coal and various

metals for the mass production of goods, it was quickly clear

that it caused terrible _____

_____[2], poisoning land, air and water in the

area. However, it now seems that human activities are also

causing much wider damage. Burning fossil fuels is

producing _____[3] in the form of gases, and these

_____[4] are raising worldwide temperatures. This is

_____[5], and it appears to be leading to _____

_____[6], which is likely to have disastrous effects on the world's weather systems.

2 GETTING IT RIGHT

→ Participles, SB S. 267

Expand and connect the notes. Use the words in column 1 followed by participle clauses.

1	While	(grow up) / London	Joe Dean (love) going / help / aunt & uncle on / farm in / country / school holidays
2	Then before	(go) / college / age / 18	(spend) / summer as / volunteer on / organic farm
3	While	(study) economics for / next three years	(take) summer gardening jobs / make money
4	Before	(get) / 'proper' job at / end of college	(volunteer) / six months at CEFS (Centre for Eco-friendly Farming Studies)
5	Then after	(join) / big financial organization / London	(specialize) / investing in environmentally-friendly agriculture
6	After	(continue) with / work / several years	(start) dreaming / leaving & running / own project
7	Then while	(visit) / aunt & uncle, now in their 60s,	(begin) talking / his ideas & they (invite) him / run / farm for them
8	Since	(take over) / aunt & uncle's farm	(introduce) organic farming & / lot / new techniques

Start like this: *While growing up in London, Joe Dean loved going to help his aunt and uncle on their farm in the country in the school holidays. Then before ...*

3 GETTING IT RIGHT

→ Participles, SB S. 267

Change the relative clauses (starting with *who, which, that*) to *~ing* or *~ed* clauses. Start like this:
For over 200 years, there have been people saying that famine would soon kill millions and ...

For over 200 years, there have been people who have said that famine would soon kill millions and who have predicted a great reduction in the human population. For example, enormous
5 famines that were predicted in the 1950s for India* and other parts of the world did not happen. Certainly, the scenes of African starvation which have often been shown on our TV screens have been real and terrible enough.
10 However, the fact is that scenarios which warned of hundreds of millions of deaths have not come true – at least, not yet.

This is largely thanks to a green revolution that was created just in time by new varieties of
15 rice, wheat and other crops. These are varieties that were developed by selective breeding in the 1960s and that produce far more food per acre with much greater reliability than before.

However, the productivity push that was
20 given to farming by this revolution is coming to an end, even while the population goes on rising rapidly. The race that is continuing ever more urgently today is to create a new green revolution to get us through the next half century. (190 words) 25

* See e.g. *The Population Bomb*, Paul Ehrlich, published 1968.

4 WORKING WITH WORDS

A Add these words from pages 147–157 of the student's book to the mind map.

crops ▪ disease ▪ drought ▪ fertilizer ▪ GM technology ▪ herbicide ▪ hydroponics ▪ livestock ▪ organic practices ▪ pests ▪ pollution ▪ runoff ▪ selective breeding ▪ vertical farms ▪ weeds

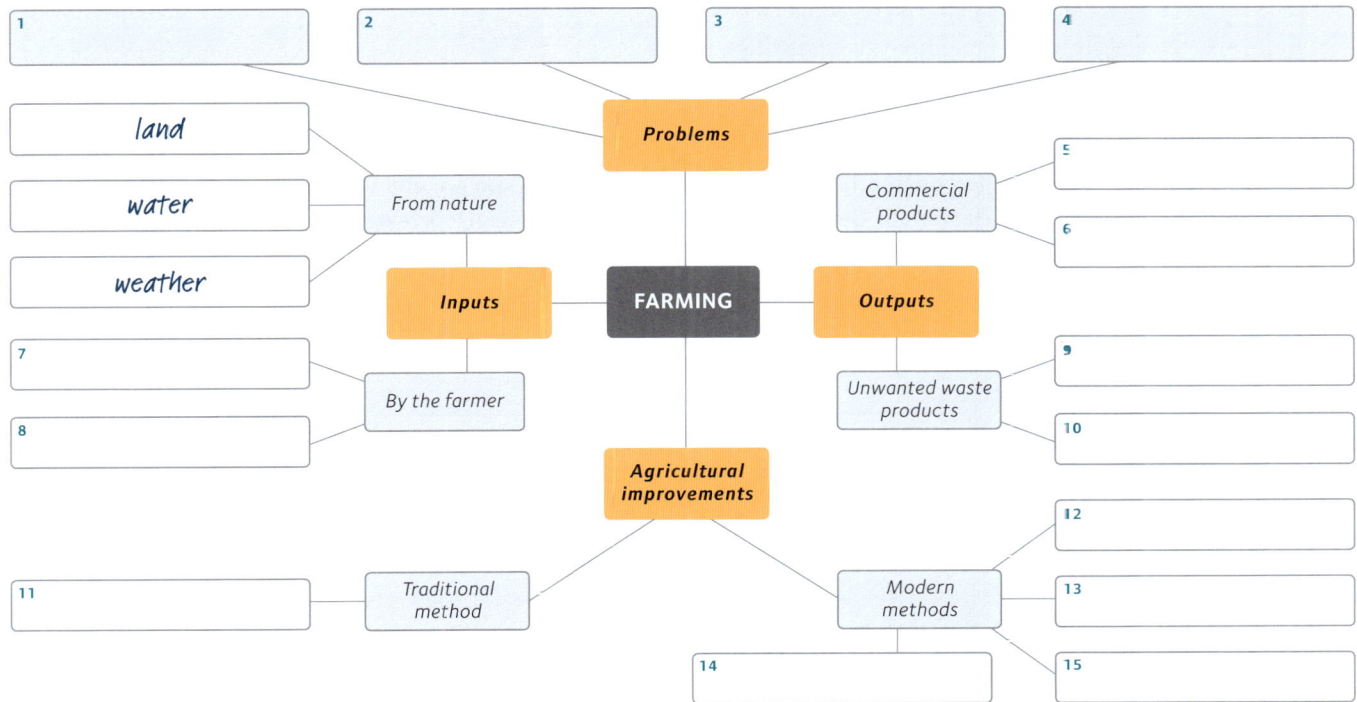

B Now complete these statements with words from the mind map.

1 Inputs to farming from nature include land, water and _____[1], while inputs by the farmer include _____[2] and _____[3].

2 There is always a danger of damage and destruction, and the farmer faces many _____[4] such as _____[5], _____[6], _____[7] and _____[8].

3 The intended commercial products of farming consist of _____[9] and _____[10], but there are also _____[11] which include _____[12] and _____[13].

5 LISTENING

Sie studieren in London und haben nicht viel Geld für Lebensmittel. Da hören Sie zufällig einen Radiobeitrag der Ernährungsberaterin Dr. Sally Carter.

EXAM
→ Hörverstehen,
SB S. 178

15

A Hören Sie den ersten Teil des Radiobeitrags aufmerksam an, und beantworten Sie anschließend die unten stehenden Fragen auf Deutsch in ganzen Sätzen.

1 Welche zwei Möglichkeiten gibt es, wenn man Hunger hat, aber nur 10 Pfund ausgeben kann?
2 Was für eine Mahlzeit schlägt Dr. Carter zunächst vor? Woraus besteht dieses Essen?
3 Wie sieht es mit dem Nachtisch aus?
4 Was könnte man laut Dr. Carter alternativ machen?
5 Was für Lebensmittel erwähnt sie?
6 Wieviel kostet diese Essen insgesamt?

16

B Hören Sie nun den zweiten Teil des Radiobeitrags aufmerksam an, und vervollständigen Sie dann die folgenden Sätze auf Deutsch.

1 Manche Menschen essen besonders gerne …
2 Zum Einen liegt das daran, dass viele diese Art von Essen einfach …
3 Außerdem wird eine Menge Recherche betrieben, damit dieses Essen besonders …
4 Zum Anderen liegt es daran, dass viele Leute nicht gerne …
5 Noch dazu gibt es einfach Leute, die nicht wissen, …
6 Vielleicht waren ihre Eltern zu beschäftigt, um es …
7 Zu guter Letzt ist diese Art von Essen, wie der Name schon sagt, einfach …
8 Für diese Art von Essen benötigt man weniger Zeit und Aufwand, als für ein …

17

C Hören Sie sich jetzt den dritten Teil des Radiobeitrags aufmerksam an, und vervollständigen Sie dann das unten stehende Raster auf Deutsch mit Informationen aus dem Hörtext. Wie viel Zeit benötigt man für beide Mahlzeiten?

Mahlzeit	Aktivität		Zeit (Minuten)	
A Fast Food	a	Hin- und Rückfahrt	15	
	b	_____	_____	Gesamt
	c	_____	_____	_____
B Haus- gemacht	a	_____	_____	
	b	_____	_____	Gesamt
	c	_____	_____	
	d	_____	_____	_____

6 MEDIATION

Auf der Intranetseite Ihrer Schule findet derzeit eine interessante Diskussion zum Thema gesundes Essen statt. Die vorherrschende Meinung ist, dass das, was wir in Deutschland essen, gründlich getestet wurde und somit definitiv für den Verzehr geeignet ist. In diesem Zusammenhang stoßen Sie auf einen interessanten Artikel im Internet über TTIP. Entnehmen Sie dem Text die relevanten Informationen, und schreiben Sie eine Zusammenfassung für die Intranetseite Ihrer Schule.

EXAM
→ Mediation, SB S. 179

What is TTIP? And six reasons why the answer should scare you

[…] Have you heard about TIPP? If your answer is no, don't get too worried; you're not meant to have. The Transatlantic Trade and Investment Partnership is a series of trade *negotiations* being carried out mostly in secret between the EU and US. As a bi-lateral trade agreement, TTIP is about reducing the *regulatory barriers* to trade for big business, things like food safety law, environmental legislation, banking regulations and the sovereign powers of individual nations. It is, as John Hilary,

5 Executive Director of campaign group War on Want, said: 'An *assault* on European and US societies by transnational corporations.'

Since before TTIP negotiations began last February, the process has been secretive and undemocratic. This secrecy is on-going, with nearly all information on negotiations coming from *leaked* documents and Freedom of Information requests. But worryingly, the *covert* nature of the talks may well be the least of our problems. […]

10 [Take food:] TTIP's '*regulatory convergence*' agenda will seek to bring EU standards on food safety and the environment closer to those of the US. But US regulations are much less strict, with 70 per cent of all processed foods sold in US supermarkets now containing genetically modified ingredients. By contrast, the EU allows virtually no GM foods. The US also has far *laxer* restrictions on the use of pesticides. It also uses growth hormones in its beef, which are restricted in Europe due to links to cancer. US farmers have tried to have these restrictions lifted repeatedly in the past through the World Trade

15 Organisation and it is likely that they will use TTIP to do so again. […]

So I don't know about you, but I'm scared. I would vote against TTIP, except … hang on a minute … I can't. Like you, I have no say whatsoever in whether TTIP goes through or not. All I can do is tell as many people about it as possible, as I hope will you. We may be forced to accept an attack on democracy but we can at least fight against the conspiracy of silence.   (342 words)

Abridged from: *The Independent Online*, 07 October 2014

Vocabulary notes

negotiation	*Verhandlung*	covert	*geheim*
regulatory barriers	*Kontrollhürden*	regulatory convergence	*Annäherung bezüglich*
assault	*Angriff*		*der Kontrollen*
leaked	*durchgesickert*	lax	*lasch, locker*

FURTHER OPTIONS

Read and then draw different sorts of charts to present the statistical information clearly.

1   Meat consumption compared: 1960 and today

In a few countries, less meat is eaten now than in 1960. For example, people in Argentina used to get about 650 calories a day from meat, whereas the figure is now down to about 580 – though still by far the highest amount in the world. However, people in most countries now consume more meat than they did in 1960. For example, Americans got an average of about 340 calories per day from meat back then, while today the amount is around 420. The change is much greater in Germany, with a rise from around 95 calories to about 350 calories daily today. The Chinese change of diet has been the most amazing of all. In 1960 the average Chinese person consumed only around 30 calories a day in meat, but today the figure is about 450.

2   Global human population growth from 1800

For many centuries, the planet's human population did not grow much and, at the time of the Black Death in the 14th century, it actually fell. However, by 1800 the world population was rising steadily. At that time it was an estimated 0.9 billion, but by 1850 it had reached 1.3 billion. The speed of growth then gradually increased further, and by 1900 it stood at approximately 1.7 billion. As the 20th century moved on the rate of increase grew ever more rapidly so that by 1950 human numbers totalled around 2.5 billion. By then, population growth had become explosive. In the next 50 years, it more than doubled to 6.2 billion.

1 WORKING WITH WORDS

Find words from pages 160 and 161 in the student's book, including the keyword (14).

1 The digital revolution has given us ▦ to information from all over the world.
2 Can I borrow your ▦ to call Ben? I've left mine at home.
3 If you become a ▦ , you'll learn how to write instructions that operate computers.
4 I can't talk now, so could you send me an ▦ with your suggestions?
5 'View' is an important ▦ . It lets you see text in different ways on your screen.
6 I don't use books much: I go ▦ to do most of my research.
7 I haven't got much cash with me, so I'll pay with my ▦ card.
8 If you want to change the print size, ▦ here at the top of the screen.
9 Send Lyn a text ▦ : it's cheaper than phoning.
10 I'm taking my ▦ with me so that I can keep working on the train.
11 At home, we get all our phone, TV and Internet services from just one ▦ .
12 Celtel built up a large ▦ of agents and engineers working across many parts of Africa.
13 The ▦ allows us to share information and communicate with anyone else anywhere.

Keyword: _____

2 WORKING WITH WORDS

A Complete the following. Use these words all starting with *re-*, meaning 'again'.

> rebuild ▪ redevelop ▪ remind ▪ reproduce ▪ rethink ▪ rewrite

1 It was embarrassing when I forgot her name again, and I had to ask her to _____ me.

2 Scientists all over the world are copying our experiments in order to try to _____ our results.

3 The fire damaged the clinic very badly, but they're going to _____ it just as it was before.

4 The digital revolution is changing Africa, and we must _____ our ideas about development.

5 These old 1960s office buildings are terrible. We should pull them all down and _____ the area as a shopping centre.

6 I produced the report before the new information came in. Now I need to _____ it completely.

B Form words that you know with these prefixes meaning 'the opposite of': *in-*, *im-*, *il-* and *ir-*.

_____ dependent   _____ legal   _____ possible

_____ formal   _____ literate   _____ regular

C Use opposites from B to complete the following.

1 **A** I suppose it'll be ___*impossible*___ [1] to contact you in Kenya.

  B Oh no, it's _____ [2] to use the Internet there now.

2 **A** Do farmers have to be _____ [1] to be able to use the iCow app?

  B No, it uses voice messages rather than text to help farmers who are _____ [2].

3 **A** Intersat is still an _____ [1] company, isn't it?

  B Yes, but it relies on other organizations in various ways. For example, it's _____ [2] on TechStar for customer technical support.

4 **A** I hear that out in the villages there were only _____ [1] visits by the community nurse two or three times a year.

  B Yes, but her visits are much more _____ [2] now – nearly every month.

5 **A** It used to be _____ [1] for farmers to sell the animals without any paperwork.

  B Right, but not anymore. That's _____ [2] now, and every animal has to have ID.

6 **A** I hate _____ [1] meetings where everyone wears suits. Do I really have to go?

  B Don't worry. They told me that this meeting would be relaxed and very _____ [2].

3 **GETTING IT RIGHT**

Each sentence contains one mistake. Underline it and then correct it.

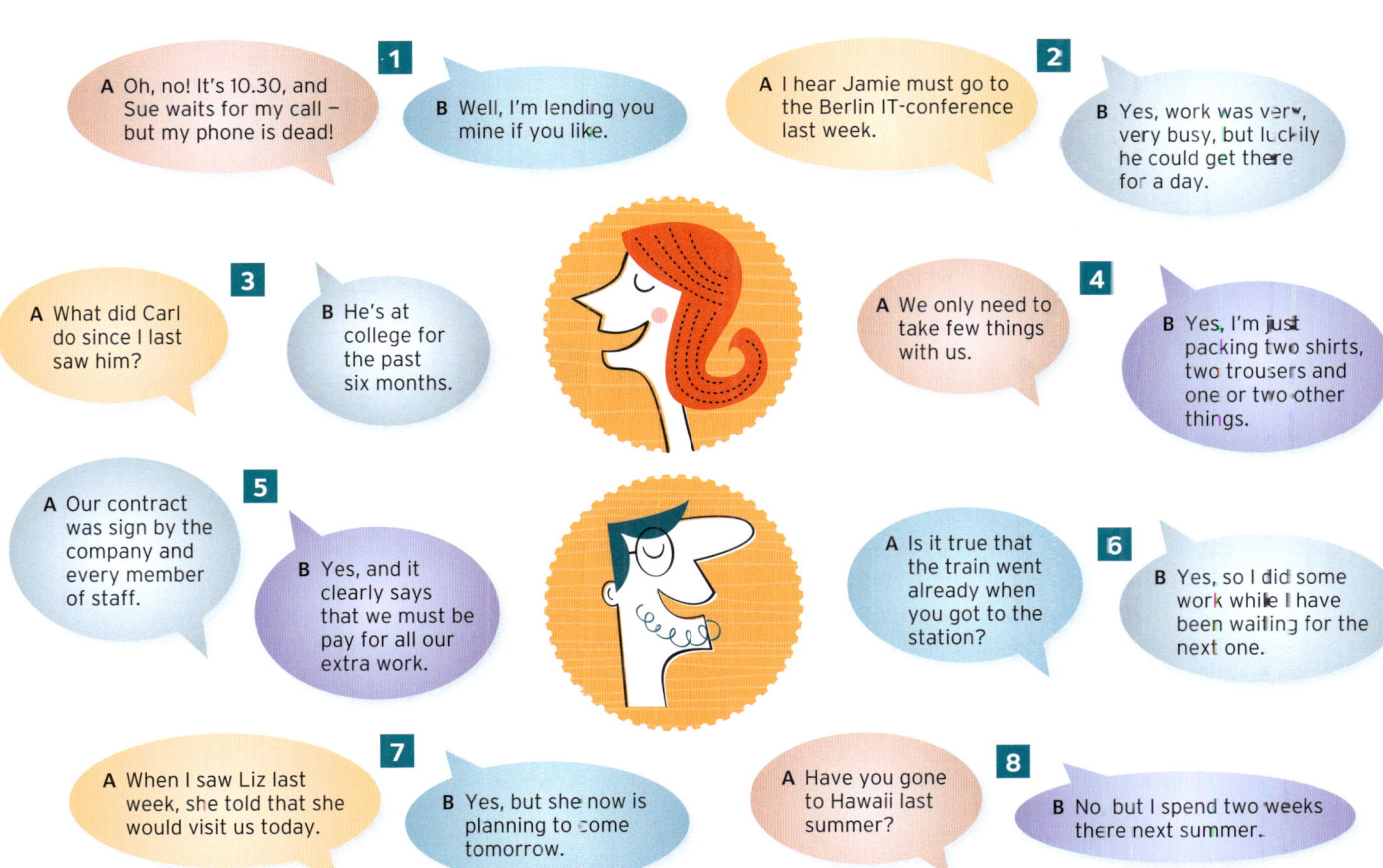

1
A Oh, no! It's 10.30, and Sue waits for my call – but my phone is dead!
B Well, I'm lending you mine if you like.

2
A I hear Jamie must go to the Berlin IT-conference last week.
B Yes, work was very, very busy, but luckily he could get there for a day.

3
A What did Carl do since I last saw him?
B He's at college for the past six months.

4
A We only need to take few things with us.
B Yes, I'm just packing two shirts, two trousers and one or two other things.

5
A Our contract was sign by the company and every member of staff.
B Yes, and it clearly says that we must be pay for all our extra work.

6
A Is it true that the train went already when you got to the station?
B Yes, so I did some work while I have been waiting for the next one.

7
A When I saw Liz last week, she told that she would visit us today.
B Yes, but she now is planning to come tomorrow.

8
A Have you gone to Hawaii last summer?
B No, but I spend two weeks there next summer.

61

4 LISTENING

EXAM
→ Hörverstehen,
SB S. 178

 18

Sie hören eine Radiosendung über fahrerlose Autos. Hören Sie aufmerksam zu, und beantworten Sie dann die unten stehenden Fragen auf Deutsch in ganzen Sätzen.

1 Welchen Beruf hat Sylvia Ray, und wo arbeitet sie?
2 Wie hat Sylvias Berufserfahrung ihre Sichtweise in Bezug auf fahrerlose Autos beeinflusst?
3 Was können fahrerlose Autos nach Sylvias Einschätzung auf den Straßen bewirken?
4 Was für positive Folgen könnte dies für Sylvia und ihre Kollegen haben?
5 Welchen Beruf hat Ben Miller?
6 Was denkt Ben über fahrerlose Autos?
7 Wie werden fahrerlose Autos den Industriezweig, in dem Ben beschäftigt ist, verändern?
8 Welchen Beruf hat Julie North?
9 Wie werden fahrerlose Autos Julies Branche verändern, und warum?
10 Was muss Julie vielleicht tun, wenn sich die Dinge so entwickeln, wie sie annimmt?
11 Welchen Beruf hat Peter Hill?
12 Warum ist er für fahrerlose Autos?

5 TEXT PRODUCTION

EXAM
→ materialgestützter
Aufsatz, SB S. 180

'Technology – a blessing or a curse?'

Write a composition. Use the information from at least three of the given materials.

1

2 The digital dump

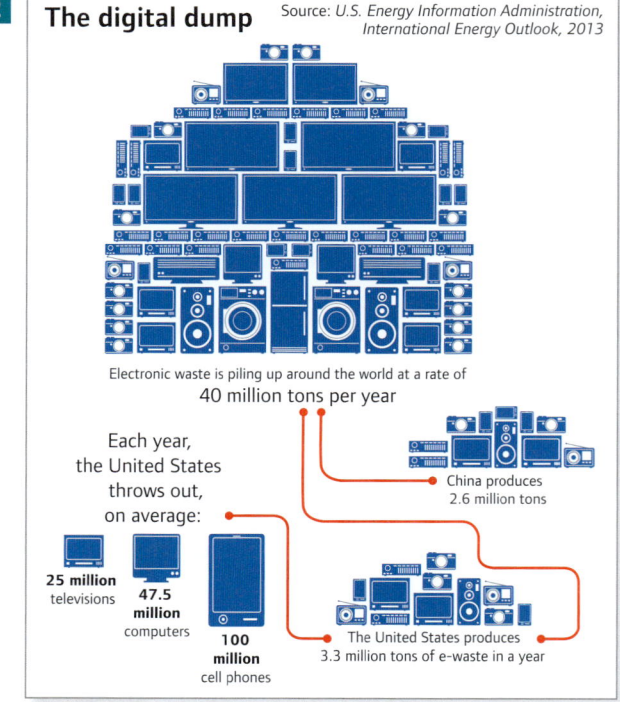

Source: *U.S. Energy Information Administration, International Energy Outlook, 2013*

3

3D printed hand gives girl new lease of life

Seven-year-old Faith Lennox never thought she needed a left hand; after all, she couldn't remember losing hers when she was only nine months old. During her birth, the flow of blood to Faith's arm was cut off and her arm was damaged [...] so doctors had to amputate just below the elbow.

5 [Faith's new hand was] custom-made in one day by a 3D printer. [...] Called a robohand, it looks a lot like the pair Marvel superhero Iron Man wears. 'It's really cool!' the otherwise shy little girl said with an exuberant grin as she stood surrounded by high-tech computers in the Build It Workspace in this Orange County suburb. Build It Workspace is a 3D printer studio that teaches people to use high-tech printers and provides access to them for projects, as well as commercial printing.

10 'It's an amazing thing to be doing,' Build It's president and founder, Mark Lengsfeld, said of making the hand from 450g of the same kind of plastic used in car parts. Children like Faith quickly outgrow expensive prosthetic limbs and have trouble even using them because of their size and weight. [...]   (186 words)

Abridged and adapted from: *The Independent Online*, 31 March 2015

4

FUTURE OF LONELINESS
in the Internet

At the end of last winter, a gigantic billboard advertising Android, Google's operating system, appeared over Times Square in New York. […] It declared: 'be together. not the same.'
5 This […] sums up the web's most magical proposition – its existence as a space in which no one need ever suffer the pang of loneliness, in which friendship, sex and love are never more than a click away, and difference is a source of
10 glamour, not of shame. […]

Behind a computer screen, the lonely person has control. […] You can filter your image, concealing unattractive elements, and you can emerge enhanced: an online avatar designed to attract
15 likes. But now a problem arises, for the contact this produces is not the same thing as intimacy. Creating a perfected self might win followers or Facebook friends, but it will not necessarily cure loneliness, since the cure for loneliness is not
20 being looked at, but being seen and accepted as a whole person – ugly, unhappy and awkward, as well as radiant and selfie-ready.   (167 words)

From: *The Guardian Online*, 01 April 2015

5

BRIEF AN DIE MASCHINEN

[…] Zusammen seid ihr uns fürchterlich überlegen. [. .] In zehn Jahren werdet ihr vielleicht schon hundertmal mehr sein als wir. Ihr werdet uns noch mehr Arbeit abge-
5 nommen haben – was vielleicht eine gute Aussicht wäre, wenn Ihr unsere Diener wäret. Doch ich werde den Eindruck nicht los, dass viele von uns eure Diener sein werden – es jetzt schon sind. Der Mensch werde zuneh-mend zu einem „Anhängsel der Maschine", beobachteten schon Marx und Engels vor über 150 Jahren.
10   Heute sind unter euch schon Genossen, die für uns planen, die uns durch den Tag coachen, uns zum Joggen ermahnen, vor fettigen Pommes warnen. Wie soll das erst werden, wenn Ihr auch noch für uns denkt? Also nicht nur rechnet, was wir Menschen nicht berechnen können, son-
15 dern abwägt und für uns Entscheidungen trefft? Einige Wissenschaftler sind dabei, euch Urteilsvermögen und eine Art Ethik beizubringen, andere wollen euch mit Emotionen ausstatten, damit ihr nicht mehr so kalt wirkt. Dagegen wäre nichts einzuwenden, wenn dieses Urteilsvermögen
20 nicht vor allem vom Militär […] benötigt würde, um bes-sere Tötungsmaschinen für das Schlachtfeld zu schaffen. Und wenn diese „Emotionen" nicht darauf ausgelegt wären, uns zu noch mehr Konsum zu verführen.   (188 words)

Abridged from: *ZEIT Wissen*, Nr. 06/2014

There are two mixed-up stories here, each with six sentences. Look for words and ideas connecting the sentences to help put them in order. Then mark them 1–6 and A–F.

FURTHER OPTIONS

1   Among them are a group from Germany who arrived very rapidly, just two days after the event. _____

2   It seemed he had escaped under it into the field beyond and, panicking, Lena called the police. _____

3   The team from Stuttgart were asked to work in an older part of town with many fallen office blocks. _____

4   After last Sunday's disastrous earthquake in Indonesia, international rescue workers have been arriving from all over the world. __*1*__

5   Frightened, she called her husband Jim, who was upstairs enjoying his hobby of model building. _____

6   Meanwhile, Jim launched his latest model, a radio-controlled helicopter with a small camera. _____

7   These spider-like machines are designed to move through small spaces using sensors to hunt for people who are trapped but still alive. _____

8   Thanks to this, they found Harry just before he jumped into the fast-flowing stream across the field. _____

9   They brought with them a number of robots to help them search collapsed buildings for victims. _____

10   Soon after letting her five-year-old son Harry play in the back garden, Lena Caine was shocked to find that he had disappeared. __*A*__

11   There, they have been using their new robotic helpers very effectively and over 50 men, women and children have already been found and rescued in the last three days. _____

12   Together, they searched everywhere until they found a small shoe outside the closed back gate. _____

Track list

Track	Title/Exercise	Page
1	Title & credits	
2	Unit 1, Exercise 7B	6
3	Unit 2, Exercise 6	9
4	Unit 3, Exercise 4	11
5	Unit 5, Exercise 4	17
6	Unit 6, Exercise 3	20
7	Unit 7, Exercise 3	25
8	Unit 8, Exercise 1	28
9	Unit 9, Exercise 5	34
10	Unit 10, Exercise 3	37
11	Unit 11, Exercise 4	42
12	Unit 12, Exercise 3	45
13	Unit 13, Exercise 4	50
14	Unit 14, Exercise 3	54
15	Unit 15, Exercise 5A	58
16	Unit 15, Exercise 5B	58
17	Unit 15, Exercise 5C	58
18	Unit 16, Exercise 4	62

Textrechte

S. 19: Mobile phones in the classroom: teachers share their tips. *http://www.theguardian.com/teacher-network/2012/sep/10/mobile-phones-classroom-teaching,* 10. September 2012

S. 19: Sollten Handys in der Schule verboten werden? *http://www.spiegel.de/schulspiegel/handy-verbot-an-schulen-sollen-schueler-smartphones-mitbringen-duerfen-a-984379.html,* 23. September 2014

S. 26: Return of the extended family home as sandwich generation take in old and young. *http://www.telegraph.co.uk/women/mother-tongue/9490940/Return-of-the-extended-family-home-as-sandwich-generation-take-in-old-and-young.html,* 22. August 2012

S. 27: Kate Mosse on the benefits of living with extended family. *http://www.dailymail.co.uk/home/you/article-1233001/Kate-Mosse-benefits-living-extended-family.html,* 12. Dezember 2009

S. 42: What makes the Tata empire tick? *http://www.independent.co.uk/news/business/analysis-and-features/what-makes-the-tata-empire-tick-10024897.html?origin=internalSearch,* 5. Februar, 2015

S. 42: Negative Folgen für den Arbeitsmarkt. *http://www.globalisierung-fakten.de/globalisierung-informationen/vorteile-und-nachteile-der-globalisation/*

S. 46–7: With the number of over-65s set to double and childcare more expensive than ever, Mehrgenerationenhäuser may be the answer. *http://www.theguardian.com/world/2014/may/02/germany-multigeneration-house-solve-problems-britain,* 2. Mai 2014

S. 54: UN-Dekade Nachhaltige Energie für alle. *http://www.bundesregierung.de/Content/DE/Artikel/2014/04/2014-04-01-un-dekade-nachhaltige-energie.html,* 1. April 2014

S. 59: What is TTIP? And six reasons why the answer should scare you, *http://www.independent.co.uk/voices/comment/what-is-ttip-and-six-reasons-why-the-answer-should-scare-you-9779688.html,* 7. Oktober 2014

S. 62: 3D printed hand gives girl new lease of life, *http://www.independent.co.uk/life-style/gadgets-and-tech/news/3d-printed-hand-gives-girl-new-lease-of-life-10147456.html?origin=internalSearch,* 31. März 2015

S. 63: The future of loneliness, *http://www.theguardian.com/society/2015/apr/01/future-of-loneliness-internet-isolation,* 1. April 2015

S. 63: Brief an die Maschinen, *http://www.zeit.de/zeit-wissen/2014/06/technologie-maschine-entwicklung-algorithmus/seite-2,* Juni 2014

FOUNDATION COURSE

Unit 1 The cult of celebrity

1 TALKING ABOUT CELEBRITY

fans, paparazzi, famous, status, star, luxury, legend, stalker, actor, image, autograph, popularity

2 GETTING IT RIGHT

1 A, 2 A, 3 B, 4 A, 5 B, 6 A, 7 A, 8 B

3 GETTING IT RIGHT

1	are	9	am scared
2	love	10	tells
3	have	11	come
4	enter	12	smiles
5	sees	13	relax
6	is not happy	14	says
7	is	15	feels
8	asks	16	win

4 ASKING QUESTIONS

1	What is/What's	4	Why are
2	Where are	5	When do
3	How do	6	Who is

5 BUILDING SKILLS

b

6 LOOKING AT THE TEXT

1 False. Desirée is last month's winner of *Stars for Tomorrow*.
2 False. Patrick is one of the judges on *Stars for Tomorrow*. (He and Desirée are in a relationship.)
3 True
4 False. She accepts that paparazzi take photos when she is not looking perfect / having a bad day.
5 False. The media is full of reports about her personal life.
6 True

7 GETTING IT RIGHT

1	am calling	6	are going too far
2	are you doing	7	Are they trying
3	am reading	8	are only doing
4	is the press making up	9	are walking up
5	are dating	10	am driving into

8 GETTING IT RIGHT

1	am working	5	are looking
2	is going	6	know
3	am having	7	believe
4	stalk	8	love

Unit 2 The world of sport

1 TALKING ABOUT SPORT

A		B	
1	participant	1	keep-fit activities
2	spectator	2	do aerobics
3	football	3	go jogging
4	play tennis	4	participant
5	support a team	5	football
6	keep-fit activities	6	spectator
7	do aerobics		
8	go jogging		

2 GETTING IT RIGHT

1	went	4	began
2	played	5	bought
3	won	6	took part

3 GETTING IT RIGHT

A
1 1 has left; 2 has just moved (signal word: just)
2 1 has not arrived; 2 has never been (signal words: yet, never)
3 1 Have you heard; 2 has just joined (signal words: already, just)
4 1 Have you met; 2 has played (signal word: yet)

B			
1	for	5	since
2	for	6	since
3	since	7	since
4	for	8	for

4 GETTING IT RIGHT

1 charged (earlier today)
2 has not said (up till now)
3 searched (earlier this week)
4 has won (during his career)
5 told (yesterday)
6 drank (before)
7 has sponsored (for)
8 said (this morning)
9 has been (for)
10 gave (before)
11 were (as always)
12 have ever contained (ever)

5 GETTING IT RIGHT

A

1 him
2 me
3 **1** She; **2** them
4 **1** us; **2** it
5 **1** They; **2** We; **3** it

B

10 subject pronouns (sp); 9 object pronouns (op);
 6 possessive adjectives (pa)

line 1 my (pa); We (sp)
line 2 Her (op); She (sp)
line 3 It (sp)
line 4 us (op)
line 5 his (pa); Its (pa)
line 6 him (op); me (op); you (sp)
line 7 I (sp); him (op); he (sp); me (op); It (sp)
line 8 we (sp); His (pa); us (op); them (op)
line 9 their (pa); They (sp)
line 10 you (sp); me (op); your (pa)

6 BUILDING SKILLS

A/B

Expressions we hear: 1, 3, 4, 5, 6, 8, 9
Expressions we don't hear: 2, 7

C

Jane:
1 does aerobics
2 home
3 heart, lungs
4 stress
5 (too) expensive

Will:
1 goes swimming
2 at local swimming pool
3 work-out
4 sleep well
5 weight
6 slim and stay slim

Lily:
1 plays volleyball
2 at college
3 lose
4 burns up
5 friends
6 get to know people
7 good friends

Unit 3   Fashion and brand power

1 TALKING ABOUT BRANDS

A

1 slogan
2 fashionable
3 price
4 product
5 affordable
6 quality
7 advertising
8 values
9 choice
10 famous

B
brand names

2 GETTING IT RIGHT

A

1 carefully
2 simply
3 beautiful
4 usually
5 similar
6 expensive; cheaply

B

1 Lucy <u>frequently</u> shops at the outlet store.
2 Jim <u>always</u> dresses well.
3 My new computer <u>suddenly</u> stopped working.
4 The coffee in that café is <u>usually</u> good.
5 I <u>really</u> want these boots.

3 USING A DICTIONARY

1 choose
2 choosy
3 cost
4 costly
5 affordability
6 afford

4 GETTING IT RIGHT

A/B

1 bigger than
2 biggest
3 lighter than
4 as heavy as
5 heavier than
6 as long as
7 longest
8 cheapest
9 more expensive than
10 most expensive
11 best
12 most difficult

C
The NeatPhone because it's the lightest and it looks the nicest.

5 COLLOCATIONS

1 low
2 victim
3 new
4 copies
5 house

6 BUILDING SKILLS

A
(Lösungsvorschläge)

Giving an opinion	(Personally,) I think / feel / believe (that) … It seems to me (that) … If you ask me, … My (own) view of the matter / problem is …
Giving reasons	You see, … The reason is (simply) (that) … The main / basic reason is (that) … The thing is, you see, …
Agreeing with an opinion	Yes, I agree. (Absolutely.) That's (quite) right / true. I couldn't agree more. Yes, that's just how I see it. That's exactly my own view / opinion …
Disagreeing with an opinion	I don't agree. (Well,) as a matter of fact, … Actually, / In fact, I think (that) … (I'm afraid) I can't accept that.
Interrupting	I'm sorry to interrupt / break in, but … Excuse me for interrupting / breaking in, but … Can I (just) stop / interrupt you there for a moment?

B

1	view	3	reason	5	afraid
2	opinion	4	disagree	6	interrupt / believe

C–E
(freie Lösungen)

Unit 4 Leisure and free time

1 TALKING ABOUT FREE TIME ACTIVITIES
(freie Lösung)

2 GETTING IT RIGHT

A

1	Will you come	5	Will I see
2	will probably be	6	won't have
3	won't be	7	will help
4	will cancel	8	will be able to

B

1 I am going to train for the next marathon.
2 Mark and Mindy are going to go backpacking in Australia next summer.
3 Some pupils are going to start a film club next term.
4 The snooker championships are going to be held in Paris this year.
5 Are you really going to buy a motorbike?
6 I'm not going to go shopping for the rest of the year.

3 BUILDING SKILLS

A

1	is lying	4	are watching	7	is standing
2	is	5	hungrily	8	angry
3	looks	6	are flying	9	is shouting

B
b

4 LOOKING AT THE TEXT

1 F, 2 F, 3 F, 4 T, 5 F, 6 T

5 BUILDING SKILLS
(Lösungsvorschlag)

Hallo …

Tut mir leid, dass du wieder Stress mit deiner Mutter hast! Ich habe kürzlich in einem Blog gelesen, dass uns allen ständig gesagt wird: „Als ich in deinem Alter war …!" Wie wahr! Die Leute, die das sagen, wissen echt, wie sie einem den Tag ruinieren …

Was diese Leute nicht verstehen, ist, dass heute eben nicht gestern ist! Wir machen ja immer noch total viel mit unseren Freunden, aber wir machen es eben anders – im Netz. Naja, ok, das ist dann nicht so direkt von Angesicht zu Angesicht, aber wir kommunizieren ja genauso viel, machen gemeinsam Hausaufgaben, tauschen Ideen aus usw. Und dabei lernen wir die ganze Zeit auch immer wieder neue Leute kennen!

Warum können ältere Leute nicht mal akzeptieren, dass sich die Welt weiter dreht und verändert? Und vielleicht sollten sie ab und zu mal darüber nachdenken, dass sie auch mal jung waren …

6 GETTING IT RIGHT

1	any	6	many	11	many
2	much	7	any	12	many
3	little	8	many	13	a few
4	a few	9	a little	14	much
5	some	10	some		

7 BUILDING SKILLS
(Lösungsvorschlag)

The photo shows a girl dressed in summer clothes, sitting on a platform next to a railway track. The tracks are in the countryside and are leading to a forest. The girl is alone, and she has a backpack and a sleeping mat with her. She is looking at a map. The activity shown is backpacking in a natural environment. The girl in the photo may have chosen this activity because she likes to be alone and free.

I would enjoy doing this activity. I love being free in the outdoors, wandering through the countryside, discovering new places. When I'm on my own, I can give all my attention to the place I'm visiting.

I would not enjoy doing this activity. Going backpacking alone in the countryside would bore me. I prefer to do things with my friends. And when we go on holiday, we want fun and action.

MAIN COURSE

Unit 5 The virtual world

1 WORKING WITH WORDS

1	Regardless	5	engage	9	exceeds
2	adult	6	isolated	10	avoid
3	several	7	poll		
4	appear	8	average		

2 BUILDING SKILLS

A
c

B
1 isolation, frustration, loneliness, felt need to use Facebook app
2 focus on the household (housework), spend more time with family (daughter)

3 GETTING IT RIGHT

1	went	6	thought	11	looked	16	rang
2	opened	7	was	12	Were	17	was
3	checked	8	found	13	did	18	left
4	found	9	didn't	14	didn't	19	understood
5	was	10	sat	15	couldn't	20	had to

4 LISTENING

A

1. Falsch. Margaret Green ruft Catherine Seale an.
2. Richtig
3. Falsch. Sie denkt, die Seales sind in London.
4. Falsch. Sie sitzt in ihrem Auto.
5. Falsch. Christopher hatte von seiner Mutter klare Instruktionen, keine Partys zu machen.
6. Richtig
7. Falsch. Ein Junge versucht über das Dach einzubrechen.
8. Falsch. Uneingeladene Gäste blockieren die Straße.
9. Richtig
10. Falsch. Die Bereitschaftspolizei hält die Leute davon ab, den Vorgarten zu zerstören.

5 GETTING IT RIGHT

1. hasn't used
2. used
3. **1** has changed; **2** made
4. **1** weren't; **2** felt
5. **1** told; **2** were
6. spent
7. hasn't been
8. has changed

6 BUILDING SKILLS

A

1. for a ban
2. background information
3. against a ban / background information
4. against a ban
5. for a ban

B

1. message
2. **1** chart; **2** important
3. **1** clearly; **2** dependent
4. **1** encourage; **2** access
5. **1** distract; **2** believe

C
(Lösungsvorschläge)

1. to become addicted to; mentally distant; to not notice what is happening around them; The cartoon shows that people can become addicted to their phones. They become mentally distant and do not notice what is happening around them.

2. more/less important than; a must-have; the minority/majority (+ plural verb); The chart indicates that the majority of teenagers between 12 and 17 in Germany have a smartphone. It has become a must-have that is more important than all other electronic devices like computers, TVs and games consoles.

3. to accompany you everywhere you go; to help you stay in touch with people; to feel lost and unhappy without it; The quote reveals that mobile phones are becoming the most important part of people's lives. It accompanies you everywhere you go, helps you to stay in touch with people and you feel lost and unhappy without it.

4. better equipped than many schools; to be pragmatic/flexible/up-to-date/modern; to be in contact with the teachers; The teacher in this text describes how smartphones are sometimes better equipped than many schools and should therefore be used to keep teaching up-to-date and modern. Phones can also be useful to keep in contact with the teachers.

5. to be distracting/annoying; to cheat in a class test; to neglect your friends; The teacher in this text believes that smartphones are too distracting. This is bad during lessons and in the breaks, where using smartphones means pupils neglect their friends. Smartphones also make it easier for pupils to cheat in a class test.

D
(Lösungsvorschlag)

There are several questions to think about when discussing whether mobile phones should be banned in schools. It is useful to begin by saying that recent statistics show that 79 per cent of teenagers between the ages of 12 and 17 in Germany have a smartphone. These phones have become a must-have that is more important than all other electronic devices such as TVs, computers and games consoles. It is clear, then, that smartphones are important to teenagers, but the question is whether they should be used in schools. There appear to be both advantages and disadvantages. First of all, I will look at the disadvantages and then the advantages and then decide whether a ban on mobile phones in schools is a good idea.

One disadvantage of mobile phones at school is that they are easy to become addicted to. If young people use them too often, they become mentally distant and do not notice what is going on around them. This is not beneficial at school where pupils are supposed to be attentive and have to learn. Furthermore, mobile phones can be distracting during breaks, and pupils can neglect their friends and not learn social skills. Another problem of mobile phones at school is that it is very easy to cheat on class tests.

On the other hand, there are some advantages to using smartphones at school. Some schools are not very well-equipped and don't have powerful computers etc. However, smartphones can do everything that computers can, and so allowing pupils to use their phones in class means that this is no longer a problem. Moreover, technology is so important in today's world that pupils need to learn how to use it properly, so banning mobiles would seem counterproductive. Another point to consider is contact with teachers. Apps on mobile phones can be used to share timetables and homework assignments, which can make organization easier at school.

In conclusion, then, it is clear that there are good reasons for a ban, but that there also reasons why a ban is not a good idea. In my opinion, the advantages of mobile phones are more important than the disadvantages, and so I believe that mobile phones should not be banned in schools. Technology is so important in society today that pupils need to learn how to control their use of smartphones and other technologies.

Natives

My grandfather sent postcards.
I have never seen the inside of a bank.
I find my way using satellite navigation.
All my photos are on my phone or online.
I don't possess a printer.
I have more than 200 books on my e-reader.

Immigrants

I go from shop to shop to find the best price.
I have a collection of old photos in a box.
I print out important emails for reference.
I love the quiet atmosphere of a library.
I believe online banking is very unsafe.

Unit 6 Advertising

1 LOOKING AT THE TEXT

1	e	3	i	5	a	7	d	9	h
2	g	4	c	6	j	8	f	10	b

2 BUILDING SKILLS

Correct order: d, f, i, h, b, j, c, l, k, g, e, a

3 LISTENING

1 Die angebotenen Produkte können bis zu 40 % billiger sein.
2 Die Angebote gelten bis kurz vor Landung in London.
3 Erwähnt werden ein Markenparfum und ein Markendeo für Männer.
4 Das Parfum kostet 40 £, das Deo 12 £.
5 Kunden können mit (Kredit/Debit)Karte zahlen, sowie bar in Pfund oder Euro.

4 GETTING IT RIGHT

A

1 I'm sure wearables will be a great success in the near future.
2 We are launching the whole range in Edinburgh on Monday.
3 Each member of my team is going to demonstrate a different sort of wearable.
4 I'm going to wear a waterproof Android watch.
5 We're having a press conference at 9 am.
6 We believe that demand for wearables will double in the next six months.

B

1 we're/I'm going to introduce
2 they'll make
3 We're/I'm going to start
4 you'll be
5 you'll see
6 is competing
7 She's taking
8 she'll win
9 we're/I'm going to ask
10 will win

5 BUILDING SKILLS

1 7 May 1946
2 10 (13 incl. MiniDisc, MP3 player and Android Walkman)
3 PlayStation network was hacked (77 million accounts compromised)

6 MEDIATION

A
Relevant: 5, 6
Irrelevant: 2, 7
Direkte Übersetzung: 1, 4
Persönliche Meinung: 3, 8

B
(Lösungsvorschlag)

Der Sony Effekt

Wenn es um Innovationen geht, die unser Leben verändert haben, taucht ein Name immer ganz vorne auf: Sony. Seit den 50er Jahre ist im Grunde jede Generation mit einer anderen Erfindung von Sony groß geworden, sei es das Transistorradio von 1955, der Triton Farbfernseher (1973) oder der Roboterhund AIBO (1999) – Walkman, CD-Player und PlayStation nicht zu vergessen.

1955 wurde aus der Firma Tokyo Tsoshiu Kogyo die Marke Sony, und als die Firma sechs Jahre später an die amerikanische Börse geht, sind die Weichen für den globalen Siegeszug gestellt.

Das Besondere an Sony ist, dass die Produkte immer wieder unsere Angewohnheiten verändert haben. Das Transistorradio erlaubte es uns außerhalb des heimischen Wohnzimmers Radio zu hören, und durch den Walkman konnten wir „unsere" Musik plötzlich überall hin mitnehmen.

Sony war auch die erste Firma, die wasserfeste Handys, Tablets und Smartwatches auf den Markt brachte. Ob diese Erfindungen unser Leben so einschneidend verändern werde, wie einst das Transistorradio, wird sich zeigen.

7 BUILDING SKILLS

1	gives	5	shows
2	has increased	6	has risen
3	rose	7	is
4	went	8	haven't stopped

Michael Jordan

disappointed → unhappy because you don't get something you hoped for

rapidly → quickly

huge → very large

achievement → success

improve → to become better

determination → not giving up when things are hard

estimate → to suggest an amount or a figure without exact data

merchandising → selling goods connected with a famous person or event

Kate Moss

skinny → very thin

raw → in its natural state, unchanged

undernourished → not getting enough to eat

curvaceous → with attractive curves

shape → form, contour

major → important

immediately → at once, without delay

rehab → treatment to stop drug addiction

Unit 7 Family and beyond

1 WORKING WITH WORDS

A

1	borrow	5	noisy
2	long-distance	6	forget
3	extended	7	together
4	criticize	8	huge

B
1 **1** local; **2** long-distance
2 **1** noisy; **2** quiet
3 **1** remember; **2** forgot
4 **1** together; **2** separately
5 **1** extended; **2** nuclear
6 **1** huge; **2** tiny
7 **1** borrow; **2** lend
8 **1** criticize; **2** praise

2 GETTING IT RIGHT

A
1 who came to England first
2 which was very poor
3 which paid very little
4 which would offer a better future
5 who was hiring workers for a UK textile company
6 who were offered jobs
7 which followed their arrival
8 who never gave up on anything

B
1 which made us decide to
2 she knew she might soon lose
3 which was doing badly
4 the company had already got rid of
5 who had to go next
6 the EU financial crisis hit very badly

7 who pushed for us to move here
8 I've been most worried about

3 LISTENING

1	Keighley	5	7 Bow Road, Wendcot
2	Carole Elisabeth	6	AL7 8NB
3	17	7	07765188399
4	13. Oktober		

4 GETTING IT RIGHT

1	were living	9	was looking for
2	weren't getting on / didn't get on	10	were
3	was cleaning up / cleaned up	11	was trying
		12	opened
4	had	13	had to
5	kept	14	was looking forward
6	were all cooking	15	looked
7	had	16	was
8	started	17	shouted / were shouting
		18	agreed

5 TEXT PRODUCTION

(Lösungsvorschlag)

Almost 36 million British adults live in the same house as another generation of their family and this situation is becoming normal. There are definitely financial benefits for some people living in extended families, but what problems can this living situation lead to?

To begin with, I would like to look at the advantages of living together with the extended family. First of all, the advantages for the increasing amount of young adults who still live with their parents seem clear. The price of housing keeps increasing and they can save money if they live with their parents – up to £331 per month according to one study. This helps explain why 14 per cent of young adults between the ages of 25 and 34 still live in the parental home. Secondly, there are benefits for older generations as well. Older people sometimes need a lot of care, but care homes cost a lot of money and aren't always the best option. Living with your children as an elderly person means both lower costs and the chance to spend time with the people you love. Furthermore, the middle generation can also benefit from this living situation. When generations live together, there are more people to share the housework, grandparents can easily help out with looking after the children and the family relationships can be strengthened.

However, there are also disadvantages to different generations living together. Firstly, although young adults living with their parents save money, the parents often have to spend more money, on average £107 per month. A further problem is not thinking about the other people's needs. It is easy for a mother, for example, to assume that the grandmother can look after the children of the family while she does other things, or for a young adult to assume that the mother will do all the cooking and cleaning. This can cause arguments.

To sum up, it seems to me that living in an extended family has a lot of advantages and will work well as long as everyone respects the wishes of the other family members to avoid the disadvantages.

(Lösungsvorschlag)

Dear Mrs Winter

We spoke last week about me moving to central London to study. Thanks again for your help. A friend has sent me a suggestion for a flat, and I would like to ask your advice.

It's a flat in Morden, South London. It takes five minutes to walk to the shops and seven minutes to walk to the underground. It then takes an hour to get to college. It's a flat on the third floor with one bedroom, and it's partly furnished (kitchen white goods only). There's a kitchen-diner and a bathroom and it costs £1,250 per calendar month.

What do you think of this offer? It would be great if you could give me your opinion or maybe suggest a better flat. I would also be really grateful if you could write back quickly because college starts next week.

Thanks for your help!
Best wishes

Unit 8 Entering the world of work

1 LISTENING

1   16
2   –
3   gemeinnützige Arbeit
4   Kunst, Englisch, Sport: Basketball und Fußball
5   Chemie, Biologie
6   Babysitten
7   Praktikum im Kindergarten, im Altersheim oder im Krankenhaus
8   17
9   Top DJ, DJ Headliner am Ultra Music Festival in Miami
10 DJ, z. B. im *Your Mum's House* Club in London
11 Sport, (Bodybuilding)
12 alle anderen Fächer, insbesondere Geschichte
13 Samstagsjob im Jeansshop; Arbeit im Tattoo-Studio
14 ein Musikinstrument lernen oder Musik studieren, Schule nicht abbrechen und Abschlussprüfung machen

2 LOOKING AT THE TEXT

A
1   one month minimum
2   €1,000 + tips + overtime
3   cottage in hotel complex
4   free
5   (keine Angabe)
6   max. €300 for return airfare from home country

B
1	application	4	tip	7	located
2	leisure	5	waiter/waitress	8	range
3	experience	6	willing		

3 WORKING WITH WORDS

1	gradual	4	downsize	7	filing cabinet
2	workforce	5	property	8	Human Resources
3	challenge	6	requires		

4 GETTING IT RIGHT

A
1	won't have	6	'll/will put
2	don't apply	7	change
3	send	8	'll/will be
4	'll/will tell	9	won't find
5	contact	10	wait

B
1	'd/would be	5	'd/would be
2	had	6	saw
3	worked	7	'd/would accept
4	'd/would deal	8	meant

5 MEDIATION

(Lösungsvorschlag)

Thema verfehlt

Einfach ist es nicht, sich zu entscheiden, mit welchem Beruf man für den Rest seines Lebens seine Brötchen verdienen soll. Aber laut der neuen Studie einer Arbeitgeberorganisation in England gehen die Wunschvorstellungen der Jugendlichen drastisch oft an der Realität des Arbeitsmarktes vorbei.

So zieht es ein Viertel aller jungen Menschen in die Medien-, Kultur- und Sportbranche. Ein Fünftel hofft auf einen Job im Gesundheitswesen, aber nur schlappe 0,4 Prozent hatten Lust auf einen Verwaltungsjob.

Das Jobangebot sieht allerdings genau umgekehrt aus: in Medien, Kultur und Sport wird nur jeder zehnte Aspirant fündig, im Gesundheitswesen nur jeder dritte bis vierte. Dafür könnten man problemlos in der Verwaltung, der Hotel- und Gastrobranche oder im Bank- und Finanzwesen einsteigen.

Schuld an diesem Missstand sind, laut Studie die Arbeitgeber selbst: Jugendlich neigen dazu, die Berufe ihrer Vorbilder anzustreben, darunter Lehrer, Schauspieler oder Polizisten. Über die Vielzahl anderer möglicher Berufe, die oft sogar gut bezahlt sind, wissen sie meist gar nicht Bescheid, weil sie diese schlichtweg aus ihrem Umfeld (Schule und Medien) nicht kennen.

Bei wachsender Jugendarbeitslosigkeit geht also der Weckruf an die Arbeitgeber: Engagiert Euch. Wenn Ihr Nachwuchs sucht, geht in die Schulen, sprecht direkt mit den Jugendlichen und bietet ihnen praktische Einblicke in die Realität Eurer Unternehmen.

1	warehouse	8	traffic jam
2	**home office day**	9	clock in
3	job-share	10	agency
4	flexitime	11	operates
5	temp	12	day nursery
6	shift work	13	plant
7	work-life balance	14	employment

Unit 9 Multiculturalism

1 BUILDING SKILLS

A/B
(freie Lösungen)

C
(Lösungsvorschläge)

1 He grew up in an Afro-Caribbean community / among Jamaicans / in an area he calls 'the Jamaican capital of Europe'.
2 He could not read or write when he left school at the age of 13.
3 The BBC poll showed that he was one of the country's most-loved poets / He was voted the UK's third most-loved poet.
4 This might surprise us because he attacks many things that are part of British culture.
5 He refused the (offer of the) OBE because he is against anything that has a connection with the British Empire.

2 WORKING WITH WORDS

A
1	performance	3	politics
2	poetry, poem	4	song

B
1	singer	5	performer
2	songs	6	performances
3	politicians	7	poet
4	politics	8	poems

3 GETTING IT RIGHT

1 If unemployment had not been so high in Britain, Tom would have found work without much difficulty.
2 If he had got a job in the UK, he would have stayed in Britain quite happily.
3 If things had gone well for him, he would not have wondered about work in other countries.
4 If he had never been to Australia, he is certain he would never have thought about working somewhere so far away.
5 If he had not looked for work there though, he would have missed the perfect job for him – as a tour guide for visitors.
6 If he had not taken a tour group up the Gold Coast, he would never have met the perfect girl for him, and champion surfer Jenny would never have become the love of his life!

4 GETTING IT RIGHT

1	had gone	9	had happened
2	gave	10	learned
3	had expected	11	had disappeared
4	had never visited	12	read
5	began	13	had been
6	was	14	explained
7	had experienced	15	had finally found
8	received		

5 LISTENING

1	1970.	7	Gesamtbevölkerung.
2	200 Millionen.	8	dieses Jahrhunderts.
3	5 Prozent.	9	31,1 Millionen.
4	6 Prozent.	10	ungefähr/ca. 313,7 Millionen.
5	226,5 Millionen.	11	40,8 Millionen Immigranten.
6	19,8 Millionen.	12	hält weiter an.

6 BUILDING SKILLS

1	rose	7	rapidly
2	under	8	around
3	almost exactly	9	approximately
4	reached	10	downwards
5	little change	11	fall
6	increase	12	less than

FURTHER OPTIONS

A
1	a	3	d	5	b	7	b
2	d	4	b	6	c		

B
(freie Lösung)

Unit 10 Helping others

1 BUILDING SKILLS

A
1	the Netherlands (or the UK)	3	Turkey and France
2	the USA	4	the UK
		5	Germany

B
1	percentage	3	place	5	column	7	twice
2	clearly	4	ranks	6	value	8	half

C
(Lösungsvorschlag)

Whereas private American individuals donate the most money to help others, their government donates the least money. The UK government is the biggest giver donating 0.72% of GNI and UK individuals are the second biggest givers with individual giving at 0.73% of GDP. While French individuals donate the least money, the French government gives twice as much as the US government with 0.41% of GNI compared to 0.19%. The Turkish government gives almost twice as much (0.42%) than private individuals in Turkey (0.23%) whereas the Australian government actually gives almost half as much (0.34%) as Australian individuals do (0.69%).

2 LOOKING AT THE TEXTS

A
1 True
2 False. They were 200 km away (from the British Embassy).
3 Not in the text

4 False. They were strong because they were taught to think of the needs of others first.
5 Not in the text
6 False. They were inspired by Gandhi, who always wore flip-flops.
7 False. It's a registered charity.
8 True

B

1	siblings	5	humanitarian
2	advice	6	orphanages
3	hitchhiked	7	survival
4	strength	8	charity

3 LISTENING

1 Falsch. Die Welle erreichte das Hotel nicht.
2 Falsch. Eine Million Menschen in Sri Lanka waren obdachlos.
3 Richtig
4 Falsch. Sie können Bücher von den Bibliotheken der Stiftung *Rebuilding Sri Lanka* ausleihen.
5 Richtig
6 Falsch. Die Stiftung ermutigt Kinder zur Schule zu gehen, indem sie ihnen kostenlose Verpflegung gibt.
7 Falsch Die Stiftung hat ein Zentrum für traumatisierte Kinder.
8 Richtig

4 GETTING IT RIGHT

A

1	I've [have] asked	9	She hasn't fallen
2	Have I asked?	10	We've [have] felt
3	I haven't asked	11	Have we felt?
4	You've [have] driven	12	We haven't felt
5	Have you driven?	13	They've [have] worn
6	You haven't driven	14	Have they worn?
7	She's [has] fallen	15	They haven't worn
8	Has she fallen?		

B

1 I've [have] been asking
2 Have I been asking?
3 I haven't been asking
4 You've [have] been driving
5 Have you been driving?
6 You haven't been driving
7 She's [has] been falling
8 Has she been falling?
9 She hasn't been falling
10 We've [have] been feeling
11 Have we been feeling?
12 We haven't been feeling
13 They've [have] been wearing
14 Have they been wearing?
15 They haven't been wearing

C

1	have written	6	has donated
2	have sold	7	has started
3	have been selling	8	has been working
4	has been wearing	9	's/has been serving
5	has bought	10	have bought

5 MEDIATION
(Lösungsvorschlag)

Innovatives Firmenkonzept fördert Integration

Menschen mit Behinderung haben es von je her schwer im Arbeitsmarkt. Wenn diese Behinderung mental und noch dazu schwer verständlich ist, wie bei Autisten und Asperger-Patienten, tun sich die meisten Arbeitgeber extrem schwer.

Nun stellt eine deutsche Firma unter Beweis, dass dies nicht so sein muss. Seit 2011 beschäftigt Auticon ausschließlich Software Consultants, die am Asperger-Syndrom leiden. Denn diese Menschen haben ein außergewöhnliches mathematisches und logisches Denkvermögen und sind somit prädestiniert, schnell und zuverlässig Fehler zu finden – zum Beispiel in Computercodes oder Firmenbilanzen.

Das Unternehmen ist mittlerweile profitabel und hat bereits Aufträge von Global Playern wie Vodafone und Telekom erhalten. Die Auticon-Consultants erhalten zudem Unterstützung in Sachen zwischenmenschlicher Kommunikation.

Die Idee für das Geschäftskonzept kam Firmengründer Dirk Müller-Remus übrigens durch private Umstände: Er hat selbst einen Sohn, der am Asperger-Syndrom leidet.

FURTHER OPTIONS

1	collapsed	5	donor	9	performed
2	rushed	6	miracle	10	kept
3	discovered	7	organ		
4	transplant	8	sign		

Unit 11 Global reach

1 WORKING WITH WORDS

A

1	an order	3	contact	5	action
2	a contract	4	quality		

B

1	made a mistake	5	raise a question
2	fills a need	6	take advice
3	take place	7	lose sight of
4	lost heart	8	raise our prices

2 GETTING IT RIGHT

A

1 Coffee is grown organically by farmers from all over the Gumutindo district.
2 Then the coffee is brought to the new central production facility.
3 There, quality and quantity are checked by highly-trained senior staff.
4 Then the raw coffee is processed in carefully-controlled conditions.
5 After that, the coffee is packed by the Cooperative's new, automated equipment.
6 Finally, the finished product is sent to Mombasa for export to Europe and America.

B

The ACE FURNITURE factory here in Virginia has been closed by the company owners in New York, and 200 workers have been thrown out of their jobs. The decision was made last summer, but the workforce was not told till last month. All the equipment from the Virginia plant will be sent to a new factory in Indonesia, and the same furniture will be produced there for a quarter of the pay.

But when production is moved offshore like this, American jobs are exported, too, and the American economy is damaged. If every US factory is closed, the US economy will be completely destroyed. Then who will all those 'made in Asia' products be bought by?

3 BUILDING SKILLS
(Lösungsvorschlag)

The cartoon shows a manager and one of his workers in the manager's office. He is sitting at his desk, and he is telling his employee that he is going to fire him. He is explaining that the employee has been replaced by someone in China who is better at his job and who is also cheaper to employ.

This is an ironic comment on globalization's effects on ordinary working people's lives in the West. It reminds us that the developed economies are no longer competitive with economies in the Far East, and that many US and European jobs have been exported to the developing world. Because of this, Western workers are faced with an uncertain future in the world of work.

The manager is sitting comfortably, and he is talking to the other man apparently without any sympathy. The cartoonist is attacking the way that business destroys people's lives without any human feeling. As far as the manager is concerned, the employee is just a piece of equipment that he is replacing with a better piece of equipment.

4 LISTENING

1 einem langsamen Start / einer langsamen Anlaufphase/Startphase.
2 500kg (im Monat).
3 (wieder) auf null sanken.
4 zum/am Ende des Jahres.
5 1.500kg (im Monat).
6 verarbeitetem Kaffee.
7 einen leichten Anstieg (der Verkäufe).
8 (stark/schnell) zugenommen/zugelegt.
9 1.400kg (im Monat).
10 800kg (im Monat).

5 TEXT PRODUCTION
(Lösungsvorschlag)

Globalization is something that has been affecting the world for a long time. Many people believe that this only ever benefits rich countries and causes problems for poor countries, but is this really the case?

We all know that outsourcing factories is not always a good thing for developing countries. Employees there earn very low wages and have bad working conditions,

long working hours and no social insurance. Child labour is also often a problem. This is not acceptable, of course, but although there is a long way to go, globalization has still caused improvements here. The wages may still be low, but they have increased and given people in developing countries more spending power. In fact, in most years between 1990 and 2010, the GDP (Gross Domestic Product) in developing countries saw a higher percentage rise than the worldwide economy. The two highest annual changes were in 1992 (8.5% for developing countries compared to 4.2% worldwide) and 2007 (8.4% for developing countries compared to 5% worldwide). In fact, in 2009, when worldwide development saw a decline of 1.4%, the GDP of developing countries grew by 1.6%. This must prove that globalization cannot be completely bad for poorer countries.

Further to this, it could be said that these changes in the labour market have caused problems in developed countries as well. When jobs are outsourced to developing countries, people who have been doing those jobs in the rich countries have no work anymore because someone on the other side of the world can do the same job for a much lower price. This leads to higher unemployment in developed countries, although some people believe this is partly due to technological processes and not just globalization.

So we can say that globalization has had some positive and negative effects on both richer and poorer countries. One last example of globalization that benefits both the developed and the developing world is Tata, the Indian car manufacturer. Tata has taken over many British brands to become the biggest manufacturer in the UK. This is good for the Indian company, who managed to turn losses into profits, and the UK where it now employs more than 60,000 people and has invested more than £12 billion in the British economy since 2000. This final example shows perfectly that globalization does not only just bring benefits to the people and companies in rich countries.

FURTHER OPTIONS

| 1 | c | 3 | h | 5 | e | 7 | a |
| 2 | f | 4 | b | 6 | d | 8 | g |

Unit 12 Changing society

1 WORKING WITH WORDS

A
daytime TV, entry-level job, job application, middle management, minimum wage, pay packet, production assistant, retail industry, university degree, welfare system

B

1 minimum wage
2 retail industry
3 production assistant
4 middle management
5 welfare system
6 entry-level job
7 university degree
8 job applications
9 daytime TV
10 pay packet

2 GETTING IT RIGHT

A

1	needn't	5	must	9	may
2	should	6	shouldn't	10	might
3	can	7	can't		
4	don't have to	8	have to		

B

1 **1** haven't been able to; **2** can
2 **1** could; **2** couldn't
3 **1** can't; **2** was able to
4 **1** couldn't; **2** was able to

3 LISTENING

A

1 83
2 2
3 Er kam nicht mehr alleine klar.
4 Lucy, starb vor 12 Jahren
5 3 Kinder (2 Söhne, 1 Tochter) und 6 Enkel
6 von 2 bis18
7 Malklasse, Musik (Jazz), Tagesausflüge
8 schön dort, aber gut, auch mal raus
  zu kommen

B

1 **1** T, **2** F, **3** F, **4** F, **5** T, **6** F, **7** T

2 Er lebte 10 Jahre lang allein bevor er nach
  Windsor Park zog.
3 Er zog nach Windsor Park, weil es schwer
  wurde, alles selbst zu machen.
4 Seine beiden Söhne und die Tochter haben
  alle Kinder.
6 Sie sind mit ihm in ein Restaurant gegangen.

4 BUILDING SKILLS

a 2   **b** 6   **c** 1   **d** 5   **e** 3   **f** 4

5 MEDIATION

(Lösungsvorschlag)

Wohnmodelle für eine alternde Gesellschaft

Kann man dem demographischen Wandel auch etwas
Positives abgewinnen? Man kann, wie sich in den
Projekten der Mehrgenerationenhäuser zeigt. In diesen
Häusern kommen mehrere Generationen zusammen,
vom Säugling bis zum Rentner, um sich auszutauschen
und gegenseitig zu helfen. In manchen Mehrgeneratio-
nenhäusern kann man sogar zusammen leben, ähnlich
wie in einer Studenten-WG, nur dass man hier auch
einfach mal die Tür zu machen kann, wenn es einem
mit den Anderen zu viel wird.

Der rein finanzielle Vorteil dieser Wohnprojekte liegt
auf der Hand: Die Kosten für Altenpflege sowie Kinderbetreuung werden gleichzeitig reduziert. Aber es
geht um weit mehr: Überforderte Eltern werden ent-
lastet, weil sie Unterstützung bei der Kinderbetreuung
erhalten; Pensionisten freuen sich, unter Leute zu
kommen; und Jugendliche geben ihr Wissen über die
moderne Welt, wie z. B. den Gebrauch von Handys oder
Computern, an ältere Generationen weiter. Sogar Menschen mit Demenz sind in den Mehrgenerationenhäuser
gut integriert, weil Kinder sich ihnen ohne Scheu nähern.

Solange die Bewohner der Anlagen weiterhin selbst-
bestimmt leben können und die Interaktion auf frei-
williger Basis geschieht, bieten Mehrgenerationenhäuser
ganz klar eine Win-win-Situation für alle Beteiligten.
Dieser Nutzen ist auch den verantwortlichen Politikern
klar, nur besteht hier noch weiterer Handlungsbedarf,
denn gemäß einem Bericht der Bundregierung wird im
Jahr 2060 jeder dritte Bundesbürger über 64 sein. Bis
dahin müssen noch eine Menge neuer Mehrgeneratio-
nenanlagen entstehen.

FURTHER OPTIONS

(Lösungsvorschlag)

Mark Carter was born in 2000, and he will probably
live to the age of 80 or 90. He lives with his parents
and (one) sister in a three-bedroom house just outside
Birmingham. He is growing up with a normal early
21st-century education of two years at nursery school
and thirteen years at state school, and probably also
three or four years at university. As for employment, he
will have many options, but he may become a software
designer. The farthest that he has so far travelled is to
Florida in the USA, and he went there by plane.

Mark's life is very different from that of his great-grandfather Jack. Jack Carter was born in 1900, and he died in
1970. He lived with his parents and his six brothers and
sisters in a small terraced house in central Birmingham.
He grew up with a normal early 20th-century education
of eight years at state school and also two years of
night classes at a technical college. As for employment,
he became a car mechanic. The farthest that he ever
travelled was to London, and he went there by train.

Mark's life is even more different from that of his great-
grandfather Jack's own great-grandfather Will. Will
Carter was born in 1800, and he died in 1850. He lived
with his parents and his eleven brothers and sisters in
a small farm cottage in a village ten miles from Birmingham. He grew up with a normal early 19th-century
education of one year at the village church school. As
for employment, he became a farm worker. The farthest
that he ever travelled was to the new industrial town
of Birmingham, and he went there on foot.

EXAM PREPARATION

Unit 13 The challenges of the modern state

1 LOOKING AT THE TEXT

A
b

B

(Lösungsvorschläge)

1 Young girls are leaving the UK to become jihadi
  brides in the Middle East. They run away from
  home and seldom come back.

2 They have launched a campaign called 'Making A Stand' to stop young girls from running away. (The campaign includes a letter describing the conditions the girls will live under in an ISIS caliphate.)

3 According to the ISIS leader, a young Western woman can expect a new life and a chance to contribute to the creation of a pure Islamic state. Women can expect a variety of jobs and responsibilities, such as joining the all-female moral police force to make sure women keep to the specific ISIS interpretation of Sharia law.
According to *Making A Stand*, a young woman can expect to be married from the age of 9 and to be kept veiled and out of sight. She can expect to be treated as a second-class citizen, and to lose her individuality and dignity. She will be unable to either fulfil her dreams in the caliphate or return to the West.

4 A young woman might have been born in the UK and have enough money, but still feel socially isolated. She might suffer from depression and feel like she doesn't belong in the West because of restrictions on how Muslims can practise their religion. A young woman might decide to run away and become a jihadi bride because of personal and political reasons, but also because of naive romanticism.

2 MEDIATION
(Lösungsvorschlag)

Liebe Redaktion des Allgemeinen Tagblattes,

Würden so viele junge Menschen nach Syrien auswandern und sich extremistischen Gruppen anschließen, wenn sie genau wüssten, was sie dort tatsächlich erwartet? Ist es nicht wahrscheinlich, dass diese jungen Menschen mit einer übergroßen Portion Idealismus und naiv-romantischer Vorstellungen auswandern und, einmal im Kalifat angekommen, einfach nicht mehr zurückgelassen werden?

Würde eine junge muslimische Frau sich wirklich freiwillig dem rigorosen IS-Kalifat unterwerfen, wenn sie wüsste, dass dort Frauen ab neun Jahren verheiratet werden, verschleiert rumlaufen und der Gesellschaft fernbleiben müssen? Dass sie ihre Identität und Freiheit verlieren und zu Bürgern zweiter Klasse degradiert werden? Dass man sie dort weder mit Würde noch Respekt behandeln wird?

Studien aus England zufolge spielen vor allem depressive junge Frauen der Mittelschicht, die sich sozial isoliert fühlen, mit dem Gedanken, auszuwandern, also Frauen, die Gewalt und Krieg nie am eigenen Leib erfahren haben. Diese jungen Menschen haben oft auch das Gefühl, im Westen ihre Religion nicht frei ausleben zu dürfen und fühlen sich von dem Gedanken angezogen, dabei mitzuhelfen, einen islamischen Staat zu erschaffen. Natürlich entsprechen die Träume dieser jungen Frauen in keinster Weise der Realität, die sie in Syrien erwartet – und genau das müssen wir ihnen dringendst nahebringen!

3 WORKING WITH WORDS

A
1 terrorist
2 remind
3 succeed
4 fulfil
5 freedom
6 treat
7 dignity
8 promise
9 migrant
10 violence
11 restriction
12 practise

B
1 fulfil
2 terrorists
3 freedom
4 restrictions
5 practise
6 dignity
7 reminds
8 succeed
9 treat
10 violence

4 LISTENING
(Lösungsvorschläge)

1 sie eine von vielen wichtigen Informationsquellen sind.
2 sie oft an Orten aufgestellt werden, wo man sie nicht braucht, z. B. in Schulen und Krankenhäusern.
3 persönliche Sicherheit und Privatsphäre.
4 sie der Polizei unterstellt, das Gesetz zu brechen.
5 auf der letzten Demonstration berittene Polizei gegen die Studenten eingesetzt wurde.
6 er behauptet, dass Kameras dem Verbrechen vorbeugen, obwohl er sich selbst vor laufender Kamera mit einem Paparazzo geprügelt hat.

5 GETTING IT RIGHT

1 to open
2 to download
3 to shop
4 giving
5 doing
6 to provide
7 using
8 changing
9 to be
10 to have / having
11 to lose
12 having

6 BUILDING SKILLS

1 If you ask me
2 The main reason is
3 What's your view on
4 I couldn't agree more
5 Well, as a matter of fact
6 I'm afraid I can't accept
7 I see what you mean (or: There's some truth in what you say)
8 there's some truth in what you say (or: I see what you mean)
9 Let me put it in another way
10 do you see what I mean
11 So is the basic idea that
12 I'm sorry to interrupt, but

FURTHER OPTIONS

A

classified material, death toll, diplomatic cables, geographical area, global proportions, household name, mass surveillance, natural disasters, recent epidemic, uncontrolled outbreak, volcanic eruptions, warning systems

B

1 diplomatic cables
2 recent epidemic
3 geographical area
4 natural disasters
5 uncontrolled outbreak
6 death toll

Unit 14 Energy and the environment

1	lift	4	stop	7	opportunity
2	hugely	5	appear		
3	reason for	6	grew		

2 GETTING IT RIGHT

A

(Lösungsvorschlag)

Sally Miller stated that climate change was nothing new because it was happening all the time: it always had (done), and it always would. So she didn't think that the Greens could blame humans for something that was just part of nature.

Mark Farina did not agree. He pointed out that there was a clear connection between the rise in CO_2 levels that had begun with the Industrial Revolution and the warming that the world had seen since then. He went on to say that the more CO_2 people threw into the atmosphere, the more temperatures would continue to rise.

B

1 Kate asked if/whether her newspaper often sent her on jobs like that.
2 Chris wanted to know how long she had been away.
3 Lisa wondered if/whether she had interviewed anyone interesting.
4 Ellie inquired what she had talked to Matt Radley about.
5 Tom asked if/whether he had answered her questions properly.
6 Jean inquired if/whether she had written her report yet.
7 Tom wanted to know when they could read it in the paper.
8 Ben wondered where she thought they would send her next.

C

The Brussels trip had been Julie's first big job, so her editor Tony Good wanted a meeting about it. He called Julie and told her to come to his office for a chat as soon as she was free. Julie asked him to give her a bit longer so that she could finish her report. So Tony gave her a time, and he also requested her to email him the report before she came to let him have a quick look at it. Julie agreed, and then she asked him to (perhaps) suggest ways she could improve it.

Before the meeting, Tony contacted the Features Editor, Tania Ray, and invited her to come to his office to discuss Julie Branson's report. Both the editors liked the report, but Tony advised Julie to reduce it by about 100 words so that they could include a visual. Then he called Alan Carter in the Art Department and instructed him to prepare a visual that would show the fracking process. Finally, at the end of the meeting, Julie made a big request. She begged Tony to send her to find out how local people felt about the fracking project.

3 LISTENING

(Lösungsvorschläge)

1 Sie findet es verrückt, weil wir bereits wissen, dass der Klimawandel langsam außer Kontrolle gerät.
2 Man sollte stattdessen in erneuerbare Energien investieren (um die Welt zu retten).
3 Stella King macht sich Sorgen um den Lärm und die Gefahren, wenn große Lastwagen Tag und Nacht die engen Straßen passieren.
4 Besondere Sorgen macht sie sich um die Kinder.
5 Lyn Benson ist für das Projekt, weil man versprochen hat, im Gegenzug Geld in die Kommune zu investieren.
6 Brian Fox denkt, dass erneuerbare Energien den Energiebedarf für viele Jahre noch nicht allein decken können.
7 Nach Brians Meinung ist Gas wesentlich sauberer als Kohle.
8 Laut Alan Smith werden vor allem die Leute von dieses Projekt profitieren und daran verdienen, die bereits reich sind, während die lokale Bevölkerung nichts davon hat – außer Ärger.
9 Bob Lowe sagt, dass es für ein paar Monate etwas Schwierigkeiten und Lärm geben wird, aber danach wird die Produktion ohne weitere Probleme für lange Jahre rollen.
10 Bob könnte einen Job bekommen.

4 TEXT PRODUCTION

(Lösungsvorschlag)

Energy consumption is a growing problem. There are already 1.3 billion people without electricity in the world and the demand for energy keeps increasing. In fact, by 2050 there will be an extra 2 billion people on the planet, who will all want energy from somewhere. The International Energy Agency estimates that this will cost $38 trillion. However, this is just the financial cost. While providing all of this energy, we also need to think about the costs to the environment and try and cut down pollution at the same time. How is it possible to satisfy energy needs and protect the planet?

One solution to the problem is to move away from fossil fuels, which cause a lot of pollution. Statistics show that this is happening steadily with oil use, for example, which is decreasing in many countries. Usage went down by 5% in America, by 4% in Germany and the UK and by 10% in Saudi Arabia between 2008 and 2009. These, however, are all developed countries, and if we look at usage in most developing countries, oil usage is increasing, for example in India, where it increased by 4%, or Peru, where it increased by 9%. There is clearly a step in the right direction in the developed countries, and they are putting pressure on other countries to cut use of fossil fuels as well. However, this may be considered unfair, as the developing world has already left behind a huge carbon footprint, whereas the developing world still needs a lot of energy to develop their economies.

In my opinion, the solution seems to be to encourage everyone to use renewable energy. In that way, we cut down on pollution and the developing world still gets the electricity it needs to continue to grow. Experts are sure that renewable sources would be able to provide for our energy needs. The International Panel on Climate, for example, believes that 77% of the world's energy can come from renewables by 2050. The cost of this 'clean energy' is also falling, so nothing really stands in the way of providing energy for the world in an environmentally-friendly way.

FURTHER OPTIONS

A

(freie Lösung)

B

(möglicher Anfang)

I am happy to say that I support the idea of providing free bicycles for all to use across the city. I believe it would offer useful benefits – and at a very reasonable cost. I am also happy to support …

Unit 15 Feeding the world

1 WORKING WITH WORDS

A
1 greenhouse gases
2 climate change
3 environmental pollution
4 global warming
5 natural resources
6 carbon emissions

B
1 natural resources
2 environmental pollution
3 carbon emissions
4 greenhouse gases
5 global warming
6 climate change

2 GETTING IT RIGHT

While growing up in London, Joe Dean loved going to help his aunt and uncle on their farm in the country in the school holidays. Then before going to college at the age of 18, he spent the summer as a volunteer on an organic farm. While studying economics for the next three years, he took summer gardening jobs to make money. Before getting a 'proper' job at the end of college, he volunteered for six months at CEFS. Then after joining a big financial organization in London, he specialized in investing in environmentally-friendly agriculture. After continuing with this work for several years, he started dreaming of leaving and running his

own project. Then while visiting his aunt and uncle, now in their sixties, he began talking about his ideas, and they invited him to run their farm for them. Since taking over his aunt and uncle's farm, he has introduced organic farming and a lot of new techniques.

3 GETTING IT RIGHT

For over 200 years, there have been people saying that famine would soon kill millions and predicting a great reduction in the human population. For example, enormous famines predicted in the 1960s for India and other parts of the world did not happen. Certainly, the scenes of African starvation often shown on our TV screens have been real and terrible enough. However, the fact is that scenarios warning of hundreds of millions of deaths have not come true – at least, not yet.

This is largely thanks to a green revolution created just in time by new varieties of rice, wheat and other crops. These varieties developed by selective breeding in the 1960s produce far more food per acre with much greater reliability than before.

However, the productivity push given to farming by this revolution is coming to an end, even while the population goes on rising rapidly. The race continuing ever more urgently today is to create a new green revolution to get us through the next half century.

4 WORKING WITH WORDS

A
1–4 disease, drought, pests, weeds
5 + 6 crops, livestock
7 + 8 fertilizer, herbicide
9 + 10 pollution, runoff
11 selective breeding
12–15 GM technology, hydroponics, organic practices, vertical farms

B
1 weather
2 fertilizer
3 herbicide
4 problems
5–8 disease, drought, pests, weeds
9 +10 crops, livestock
11 unwanted waste products
12 + 13 pollution, runoff

5 LISTENING

A
1 Wenn man nur 10 Pfund ausgeben kann, kann man Fast Food essen oder sich etwas (Frisches) kochen.
2 Zunächst schlägt Dr. Carter ein Fast Food Essen vor, das aus zwei Hamburgern, zwei Portionen Pommes und zwei mittelgroßen Colas besteht.
3 Für einen Nachtisch reicht das Geld nicht.
4 Alternativ könnte man im Supermarkt einkaufen (und sich etwas kochen).
5 Sie erwähnt Hühnchen, Kartoffeln, Salat, Früchte und Milch.
6 Dieses Essen kostet insgesamt 9,60 Pfund.

B
1. Fast Food.
2. lieben/mögen.
3. lecker ist/schmeckt.
4. kochen.
5. wie man kocht.
6. es ihnen beizubringen / zu zeigen.
7. schnell.
8. selbstgekochtes Essen.

C
A *Fast Food*
a Hin- und Rückfahrt: 15
b Bestellen: 5
c Essen: 15   Gesamt: 35

B *Hausgemacht*
a Einkaufen: 45
b Vorbereiten: 45
c Essen: 20
d Abwaschen & Aufräumen: 15   Gesamt: 125

6 MEDIATION
(Lösungsvorschlag)

TTIP – Igitt!

Gesundes Essen in Deutschland? Das könnte bald der Vergangenheit angehören, wenn das Transatlantische Freihandelsabkommen TTIP tatsächlich kommt, wie geplant. Das Abkommen will nämlich die Sicherheitsrichtlinien für Lebensmittel den US-amerikanischen Standards anpassen – oder besser gesagt, sie auf deren Niveau absenken.

Und was ist Standard in den USA? Standard ist, dass 70 Prozent aller dort verkauften verarbeiteten Lebensmittel genetisch-veränderte Zutaten haben. Oder dass man mit Pestiziden wesentlich „großzügiger" umgeht. Wachstumshormone in Rindfleisch? Kein Problem! Selbst wenn man hier einen Zusammenhang zu Krebserkrankungen vermutet.

Und wer profitiert davon? Natürlich die Großkonzerne und kein einziger Bürger, und darum finden die Verhandlungen auch hinter verschlossenen Türen statt. Das sollten wir uns aber nicht länger gefallen lassen, denn schließlich geht es um unsere Gesundheit – und die unserer Umwelt!

FURTHER OPTIONS

(freie Lösung)

Unit 16 Technology

1 WORKING WITH WORDS

1	access	8	click
2	mobile	9	message
3	programmer	10	laptop
4	email	11	provider
5	function	12	network
6	online	13	Internet
7	credit	14	communication

2 WORKING WITH WORDS

A
1	remind	3	rebuild	5	redevelop
2	reproduce	4	rethink	6	rewrite

B
independent, illegal, impossible, informal, illiterate, irregular

C
1. 1 impossible; 2 possible
2. 1 literate; 2 illiterate
3. 1 independent; 2 dependent
4. 1 irregular; 2 regular
5. 1 legal; 2 illegal
6. 1 formal; 2 informal

3 GETTING IT RIGHT

1. is waiting / I'll (I will) lend
2. had to go / he was able to
3. has Carl been doing / He's been
4. a few / two pairs of trousers
5. was signed / must be paid
6. had already gone / I was waiting
7. told me / now she is/she is now
8. Did you go / I'm going to spend/I'm spending

4 LISTENING
(Lösungsvorschläge)

1. Sylvia Ray ist Krankenschwester, und sie arbeitet in der Notaufnahme/Notfallambulanz.
2. Sylvia sieht täglich die schrecklichen Ergebnisse von (Auto)Unfällen, die durch menschliches Versagen verursacht wurden.
3. Nach ihrer Einschätzung könnten fahrerlose Autos die Zahl der Verkehrstoten und -verletzten auf den Straßen deutlich reduzieren.
4. Sylvia und ihre Kollegen hätten dadurch mehr Zeit, sich anderen medizinischen Problemen zu widmen.
5. Ben Miller ist Direktor einer Straßenbaufirma.
6. Er hält fahrerlose Autos für eine furchtbare Idee.
7. Fahrerlose Autos könnten dazu führen, dass Arbeitsplätze in seiner Branche verloren gehen, weil keine neuen Straßen mehr gebaut werden müssten, sondern nur noch Reparaturen anfallen.
8. Julie North ist Vertreterin für Autoversicherungen.
9. Es werden geringere Prämien bei den Autoversicherungen anfallen, weil fahrerlose Autos sicherer sind.
10. Julie müsste sich vielleicht einen neuen Job suchen (oder andere Versicherungen verkaufen).
11. Peter Hill ist Beamter in der Stadtplanung.
12. Peter möchte, dass die Städte effizienter werden (indem die Anzahl der parkenden Autos reduziert wird). Da fahrerlose Autos von vielen Leuten nacheinander benutzt würden, müssten die Autos nicht lange geparkt werden, sondern könnten gleich selbstständig zum nächsten Kunden fahren.

5 TEXT PRODUCTION
(Lösungsvorschlag)

There is no question that technology is an important part of life in today's society. We are surrounded by mobile phones, the Internet, apps that tell us what to eat and when to exercise and there is always new technology on the market. The question is whether this is a blessing or a curse.

Let's first look at the ways that technology has improved our lives. One important factor is how it can help disadvantaged people who are disabled or unable to do certain things. For example, people without limbs often had to struggle in life because prosthetic limbs were just too expensive. However, nowadays 3D printing technology can use the same kind of inexpensive plastic that is used in car parts to make cost-effective prosthetic limbs that anyone can afford.

Another positive effect of technology is the Internet and how it can connect people. Families and friends that live in different countries can keep in touch and nobody needs to be lonely as it is easy to make friends online. However, this can also be a negative, as people who only interact online do not necessarily have real friendships and they will still be lonely. Furthermore, smartphones enable people to be continuously online and available. This can mean that we are constantly absent from the 'real world' and can no longer appreciate what we have, for example nature.

Another point to consider is what we do with all of our machines when we have bought the latest versions. Electronic waste is becoming a big problem with 40 million tons of electronic waste being produced worldwide each year. This is a huge amount of waste, which has a negative effect on the environment.

To sum up, I think that while technology has brought us many good things and has helped a lot of people, it can sometimes be a curse as we have become too dependent on it. In my opinion, we need to learn to not let technology control our lives.

FURTHER OPTIONS

Story 1–6
4, 1, 9, 7, 3, 11

Story A–F
10, 5, 12, 2, 6, 8

Audioscripts

Unit 1, Exercise 7B

Desirée Hi Patrick.

Patrick Hi Desirée. I am calling from my car. What are you doing at the moment?

Desirée I'm reading the latest report about us in the newspaper.

Patrick What story is the press making up now?

Desirée That you're dating another woman.

Patrick These people are going too far. Are they trying to split us up?

Desirée I suppose they are only doing their job. Oh, no! Two reporters are walking up the path to the front door.

Patrick Don't worry, darling. I'm driving into your street right now. I can see them. Hey, you!

Unit 2, Exercise 6

1

Interviewer Good morning, Jane. Thanks for agreeing to talk to our listeners about keeping fit. You do aerobics, I believe?

Jane That's right. As far as I'm concerned, aerobics is one of the best ways to stay healthy. It strengthens the heart and the lungs and it's also a great way to reduce stress. It's exactly the right thing for me after a long day at work.

Interviewer Yes. I can imagine that all those powerful moves help to get rid of stress. How often do you do aerobics?

Jane I go to a class once a week, but I also do aerobics at home. I just put on some music and do the moves.

Interviewer What would you say to anyone thinking about doing aerobics as a way to keep fit?

Jane It's a fun way to keep fit and it's not too expensive. You don't really need any special clothes and once you've paid for the class, all you have to do is get there on time, join in and have fun.

Interviewer So what you're saying is that doing aerobics offers quite a few health benefits. It's good for the heart and the lungs and the muscles. And it helps you get rid of stress. It's fun and it's not expensive so, if you're thinking of doing something to keep fit, why not do as Jane does, join an aerobics class and have fun!

2

Interviewer I've come to the local swimming pool where I'm talking to Will about swimming as a way to keep fit. Good evening, Will. Thanks for your time.

Will No problem.

Interviewer To begin with, why have you chosen swimming as a way to keep fit?

Will Well, you exercise every bit of your body and it's a great work-out. It's also a very relaxing activity, so it helps me to sleep well. The main reason why I go swimming, though, is to get slim and stay slim. I gave up sport when I left college and then I started to get fat. I've lost two kilos since I started swimming regularly.

Interviewer That sounds great, Will. It's a good work-out and helps you sleep and you're losing weight, too.

Will That's right. I'd definitely recommend swimming as a good way to keep fit. You don't have to have a great body to go swimming. People of all shapes and sizes go swimming

Interviewer Thanks, Will. Just to go over what you said: when you swim, you exercise every part of your body. Swimming helps you relax, so you can sleep well and it also helps you lose weight. So, all you listeners, if you feel you need any of these benefits, it doesn't matter what you look like, get your swimming gear on and jump in!

3

Interviewer The last person I'm talking to today is Lily. She's just finished an exciting game of volleyball Hi, Lily. How was the game?

Lily My team didn't win, but everyone had a lot of fun. That's one of the good things about volleyball. Even if you lose a game, you still feel great afterwards

Interviewer Anything that gives you a good feeling must be good for your health. What about the other health benefits of playing volleyball?

Lily Well, it certainly burns calories. That's not why I took up volleyball, though. I've never been overweight. No, when I started college, I wanted to get to know people so I looked for a team sport. The people in the volleyball team here at college were really nice, so I joined the club.

Interviewer Team sports certainly are a good way to get to know people

Lily Definitely, every team sport helps you make friends. You're working together to get the best result and that makes you feel good, too.

Interviewer And that's another health benefit, eh? Well, listeners, what about volleyball as a way to keep fit? It's a lot of fun, it makes you feel great and it burns up calories. It's a team sport and, as Lily said, team sports help you make friends, and working together with them for a good result keeps you healthy, too. Thanks, Lily.

Unit 3, Exercise 4

Oh, dear. I'm not sure which of these three phones to choose. I can see that the Universe is bigger than the NeatPhone and the Bright is the biggest of all three, but I'll have to think some more.

How heavy are they? The NeatPhone is lighter than the two other phones. The Universe is not as heavy as the Bright. The Bright is heavier than the other two.

What does it say here about the battery life? The battery life of the NeatPhone is not as long as the battery life of the Bright. It looks as if the batteries of the Universe last longest.

What about the price? Well, the Bright is the cheapest of the phones. The NeatPhone is more expensive than the Bright and the Universe is the most expensive of them all.

Oh, I don't know which of these three phones is best. Choosing a phone is one of the most difficult things to do in life. Hmmm. I think I'll buy the NeatPhone. It's the lightest and it looks the nicest. Yes. It's the NeatPhone. That's the one I'll buy.

Unit 5, Exercise 4

Catherine	Hello?
Margaret	Oh, hello. Am I speaking to Catherine Seale?
Catherine	Yes, that's right. Who's speaking, please?
Margaret	It's Margaret Green. Your son Christopher and my son Jamie are in the same class at school.
Catherine	Ah, yes I remember! I think Jamie was at our house a few weeks ago. If you're trying to reach Christopher, please try him on his mobile because my husband and I are on holiday in France at the moment.
Margaret	In France! Oh dear! I thought you were here in London. Well, I think I understand better what's happening now because I've just brought Jamie to your house for the party and …
Catherine	Party! What party? I told him not to have any parties!
Margaret	Well, there's certainly one going on in your house at the moment. I'm in my car outside and I think it's out of control. There are young people everywhere, some are drunk and vomiting in the front garden and I think I can see someone on the roof.
Catherine	On the roof! That can't be true! Oh my god, what's happening?

Margaret	I think the boy on the roof is trying to open the skylight. I think he's trying to break in. It doesn't look good here, Catherine. There's very loud music and from what I can see they're all dancing wildly in the front room.
Catherine	On my new carpet! They'll trash it! Can't you stop them somehow?
Margaret	I'm not sure but can you hear that siren?
Catherine	Siren? You mean the police siren?
Margaret	Yes, the riot police are here now and they're breaking up all the people blocking the street and in the front garden.
Catherine	The riot police are breaking up the people blocking the street! How many are there outside the house?
Margaret	I would say hundreds. I'm so sorry to tell you all this but I think they must be gatecrashers because Jamie said Christopher only invited 60 people and was going to have a bouncer to make sure nobody else got in.
Catherine	I just don't believe this! Is my son Christopher there?
Margaret	I can't see him. He must be inside but I don't want to go in there with all those drunken revellers. Anyway, the riot police have stopped the people wrecking the front garden now.
Catherine	My husband has been listening and we're getting the first flight back to London! Thanks for letting me know, Margaret.
Margaret	Don't mention it and have a nice flight!

Unit 6, Exercise 3

We hope you're enjoying your flight with High Sky Air Travel. In a few moments, you will have the chance to take advantage of our super in-flight perfume and cosmetics prices, which are up to 40% cheaper than on the high street. Yes, you heard it right! As a passenger on a High Sky flight you have the chance to buy top brand perfume and cosmetics up to 40% cheaper! These prices are valid until just before we land in London, so this is a real chance for you to save money. For example, why not buy a 50 ml bottle of a top brand perfume for just £40 and save £15 pounds on high street prices? Or a 75 ml top brand deodorant stick for men for just £12 compared to £20 in your local store? These are just two examples of our unbelievable offers. Pay by card or cash in pounds or euros when our cabin crew come by and ask them to show you what other great deals we have for you.

Unit 7, Exercise 3

Officer	Well, Carrie, let's start with some personal details, shall we?

Carrie	Fine, yes.
Officer	So first, can I have your family name?
Carrie	It's Keighley.
Officer	Could you spell that for me, please?
Carrie	Yes. It's K-e-i-g-h-l-e-y.
Officer	Right, and your first name? What is Carrie short for?
Carrie	Carole – with an 'e' on the end. And my middle name is Elisabeth. That's spelt with an 's', not a 'z', by the way.
Officer	So your given names are Carole – C-a-r-o-l-e – Elisabeth – E-l-i-s-a-b-e-t-h.
Carrie	That's right.
Officer	And what age are you now?
Carrie	I'm 17 now. My birthday was last month. The 13th of October.
Officer	The 30th of October?
Carrie	No, the 13th.
Officer	Thanks, so that gives me your date of birth … And now can I make a note of your home address, please?
Carrie	Yes, it's 7 Bow Road, Wendcot.
Officer	OK, so that's 7 Bow Road, Wendcot. And the post code?
Carrie	It's AL7 8NB.
Officer	AL7 8NB. Good, and now your phone number?
Carrie	I'll give you my mobile, all right?
Officer	That's fine.
Carrie	It's oh-double-seven-six-five …
Officer	Oh-double-seven-six-five …
Carrie	One-double-eight-three-double-nine.
Officer	Double-one-eight-three-double-nine.
Carrie	No, sorry. That's one-double-eight-three-double-nine.
Officer	Oh, right. Good. Now, let's talk about your situation at home …

Unit 8, Exercise 1

Dialogue 1

Advisor	Good morning, Meera.
Meera	Good morning.
Advisor	Please take a seat.
Meera	Thanks.
Advisor	I'm very glad you've come, Meera, because it's a good idea to start planning your career early, and 16 is a good age to start. The first thing I'm going to do is ask you a few questions to find out what sort of person you are. Alright?

Meera	Yes, fine.
Advisor	What's your dream job?
Meera	Dream job … er … I'm not sure, really. I don't really know.
Advisor	Don't worry. Not many people can answer that question. What activities do you do outside school in your free time?
Meera	Well, I signed up for our school's community service group and we visit people who need some help. For example, there are mothers with young children who need help at home, sometimes just holding the baby or playing with the toddlers. And then there's an old man near the school who needs a bit of shopping done. That kind of thing.
Advisor	That's very helpful information, Meera. Now what about your subjects at school? Which ones do you like most?
Meera	Well, I love art! I won the art prize last year for a painting I did and it's still up on the wall in the entrance to our school as you come in. And I like English, of course. I like to read stories about what life is like for young people in other countries. That sort of thing. Oh, and I forgot sport. I like basketball and football, too.
Advisor	And are there any subjects you don't like?
Meera	Chemistry! I really don't know why we do it. Biology is hard work, too.
Advisor	Well, I'm getting a picture of you now, Meera. Do you have any work experience?
Meera	No, not really.
Advisor	Not helping out in a shop, giving out leaflets, baby-sitting or anything like that?
Meera	Oh, yes baby-sitting, of course! That's not work. That's fun.
Advisor	And do you get paid for it?
Meera	Oh, yes. I'm always being asked by friends and family. Last month I made almost a hundred pounds!
Advisor	Well, I think I have a picture of you now, Meera. I think you might like a job looking after people, young or old, so I think you should do a work placement in a kindergarten, an old people's home or a hospital and then come back to me.
Meera	A kindergarten would be nice.
Advisor	Here's a list of addresses to contact … *(fade)*

Dialogue 2

Advisor	Good morning, Christopher.
Christopher	Hi.
Advisor	Please take a seat.
Christopher	Thanks.

Advisor	I'm glad you've come to see me, Christopher, because I think 17 is a good time to think about planning your future.
Christopher	Look, to be honest I'm here because everybody in my year has to see a careers advisor when they're 17. I already know what I want to do and on my 18th birthday I'm going to walk out of school and do it.
Advisor	Before your exams in May?
Christopher	Yes. My 18th birthday's in March, so I can leave on the day I'm 18.
Advisor	That's a big decision to make, Christopher. You're doing well at school. I can see that from your good results. Do you really dislike school that much?
Christopher	It's meaningless. I see my friends there but I'm basically just wasting my time.
Advisor	So you already know what your dream job is?
Christopher	Yes, I'm going to be a top DJ and my ambition is to be a DJ headliner at the Ultra Music Festival in Miami. I don't need school for that, do I?
Advisor	I see. How much do you know about the job?
Christopher	Well, in my free time I'm a DJ. And in the holidays I had a guest DJ residency at Your Mum's House. It was great!
Advisor	And Your Mum's House is the name of a nightclub?
Christopher	Yes, it's a number one club. I've played there and they want me back.
Advisor	Well, I can see you know a lot about music and that you'are very ambitious, but I still have some questions I'd like to ask you. Is that alright?
Christopher	Fire away.
Advisor	What are your favourite subjects at school?
Christopher	None.
Advisor	Is there absolutely nothing you like at school?
Christopher	The only thing I like doing there is sport because I want to keep fit. A DJ has to look good and I like to work out. Once we did some body-building in sport and that was good.
Advisor	OK, sport and body-building and you don't like anything else at school?
Christopher	No, nothing, and of all the things I don't like, history's the subject I hate most of all.
Advisor	Alright, and apart from DJ'ing do you have any other work experience?

Christopher	I had a Saturday job in a shop selling jeans. It was alright but nothing special. And I worked in a tattoo studio. That was good and I got some cool tattoos.
Advisor	Well, I think I have a good picture of you now, Christopher.
Christopher	Good. Can I go now?
Advisor	Yes, of course, I don't want to keep you here against your will, but have you ever thought about learning a musical instrument or studying music? As you spend all your free time working with music, it would help you in your career – but you'd need to stay on at school and take your exams to study music.
Christopher	Hm, I suppose studying music could be helpful. I'll think about it …

Unit 9, Exercise 5

Presenter	Welcome to *Behind the News*. Well, US immigration is a hot political topic again, so let's take a look at it. To help us, Professor David Newman is going to talk us through the facts and figures. Well now, Professor Newman, America is a country of immigrants, isn't it? So are today's immigration numbers really so dramatic?
Newman	Well, yes and no. Way back, over a century ago, the statistics were quite similar to the figures today, so the situation now isn't new. But in between, something different happened. You see, from the early 1900s, there was a long, long fall in immigration that continued till around 1970. By that time, immigrant numbers were low – around 9.6 million out of a population of just over 200 million. That meant that the immigrant share of the population was only about 5%.
Presenter	So what's happened since then?
Newman	Well, since then, the figures have risen quite rapidly. By 1980, the number of immigrants was around 6% of the population. That was a total of 14.1 million people. And the trend continued. By 1990, the immigrant population had reached 19.8 million out of a total of just under 250 million. As a percentage, that was about 8% of the total. Then by the start of this century, in the year 2000, we see another big jump to 11% of the total population. By that time, there were 31.1 million immigrants in America.
Presenter	And more recently?
Newman	Well, in 2012, the total population was approximately 313.7 million. At the same time, the immigrant population reached 40.8 million. That was around 13% of

the whole US population. This took US immigration back to the levels that used to arrive in America around a century ago. And the trend is still rising today.

Unit 10, Exercise 3

In this podcast we'll hear how a charity set up by a survivor of the 2004 Boxing Day tsunami has provided emergency relief to people whose lives were destroyed.

Clare Allen and her daughter Daisy were on holiday in Sri Lanka when the tsunami struck. Luckily, the huge waves stopped just short of her hotel and her daughter, who had been on the beach, was found safe. The tsunami killed 40,000 people in Sri Lanka and left over a million homeless, so emergency help was desperately needed. After her miraculous escape, Clare decided to set up a charity, which she called *Rebuilding Sri Lanka*, and since then the charity has built 300 homes, a special needs school, two schools for young children, five libraries and an English language centre, to name just a few of its achievements.

One of its many projects is called 'Books and Buns', meaning education and food for children of school age. In many parts of Sri Lanka the school buildings have not been improved or repaired for decades and children who wish to pass their school-leaving exams have to pay for extra lessons and spend about £2,000 on school books. This makes it impossible for poor children to get a good education, so *Rebuilding Sri Lanka* has built modern libraries with new and up-to-date school books. Its largest library has over 2,700 members and every Saturday more than 200 books are borrowed from it.

Poor children often walk long distances to school and arrive tired and hungry, so *Rebuilding Sri Lanka* gives meals to over 5,000 schoolchildren a day. The result is a 23% increase in school attendance.

Its other projects include finding jobs for the unemployed, supporting hospitals with medical supplies and equipment and a Children's Resource Centre where traumatized children, some of whom have lost one or both parents, can receive counselling.

Rebuilding Sri Lanka is proud of the fact that its website designers, accountants and fundraisers all work for free, meaning that only 5% of the money it collects is spent on administration. 95% of donations are therefore used to help people in need.

Unit 11, Exercise 4

So now we can look back over the four years since the Gumutindo Coffee Cooperative was formed, and we can see that things have gone really well – after a slow start.

In the first half of Year 1, sales rose gradually from zero to around 500 kilos a month. They then remained unchanged at that level for the rest of Year 1. In Year 2, the change to organic production took place, and this meant a rapid fall to zero again for a short time at the end of the first half. However, organic sales then took off well in the second half, and they climbed rapidly to 1,000 kilos a month by the end of the year. In Year 3, there was a steady increase in sales to 1,500 kilos a

month by the end of the first half. This was at the same time as processed coffee production began – the now-famous Gumutindo Gold Brand. This soon affected sales of unprocessed coffee, and so there was only a slight further increase to 1,600 kilos by the end of Year 3. And this year, Gold Brand sales have really taken off. Because of this, sales of unprocessed beans declined steadily to 1,400 kilos a month in the first half, and since then, in the second half, there has been a sharp further decrease to just 800 kilos per month.

Now, Gold Brand has been a huge success story, as we all know, so let's now take a look at sales of this product.

Unit 12, Exercise 3

Carlos	Hello? Can you see me?
Peter	Yes, I can see you just fine. Hello there. And who am I speaking to?
Carlos	My name's Carlos Branco.
Peter	Well, hi. And I'm Peter North. Nice to meet you.
Carlos	And it's good to meet you too, Mr North. Thank you for agreeing to talk to me like this on Skype.
Peter	Oh, please just call me Peter. Anyway, I'm only too happy to try this Skype idea. It's nice to see a new face – especially a young one! Now how do you want to do this?
Carlos	Maybe we should tell each other a little about ourselves. Er … would you like to start?
Peter	Sure. Well, I'm Peter North, as I said, and I turned 83 years old yesterday.
Carlos	Wow! Happy birthday! And have you been at Windsor Park for long?
Peter	For about two years. Until then, I lived alone for many years, but it was getting hard to look after everything.
Carlos	Do you have any family?
Peter	Well, sadly my wife Lucy died twelve years ago.
Carlos	I'm sorry to hear that.
Peter	But I have three children – two sons and a daughter.
Carlos	And do you have any grandchildren?
Peter	Yes, six! All my children have children of their own.
Carlos	Fantastic! And what sort of ages are they?
Peter	They go all the way down from 18 to just two.
Carlos	They must be fun!
Peter	They are. And you know what? All three families came yesterday to take me out for a birthday party at a really nice restaurant. It was a big surprise. I couldn't believe my eyes when they all came through the door!

Carlos	Wow! A very special day! But tell me, what do you usually do from day to day at Windsor Park? Do you have any special interests?
Peter	Oh, yes, there are lots of things you can do here. For example, I go to an art class every Wednesday. I listen to a lot of music, too – mostly jazz. And when they organize day trips for the residents, I always try to join them. It's nice here, but you have to get out when you can.

Unit 13, Exercise 4

Host	Good evening and welcome to our live radio show *Across the country*. Our topic this evening is surveillance cameras. We've all noticed them and some of us feel safer when we see them but others certainly don't. It's estimated that there are almost six million CCTV cameras across the UK and new cameras are being installed every day, so do we just need to accept them or is now the time to do something before it's too late? Our studio guests are Detective Inspector John Langton, journalist Sally Herald, Student's Union representative Megan O'Hara and actor Johnny Pitt. We'll also be reading out your emails, texts and tweets to hear your views. Let's start off the discussion with Detective Inspector Langton. How do the police see surveillance cameras?
Inspector	The British public have the right to feel safe wherever they are, day and night, seven days a week, 52 weeks a year and we, as the nation's police force, have to make sure this happens. That's why we use everything possible to do our job. That includes surveillance cameras. Whether it's the student whose mobile is stolen, the old lady who has her handbag taken or the terrorist who leaves a bomb in a public place – we need to act fast and surveillance cameras often give us the information we need. I believe they help to make the UK a safer place.
Host	Sally Herald, as a journalist, do you share the police's opinion?
Herald	Well, I wouldn't be a journalist if I did! There's some truth in what he says, of course, but that's not the whole story. We, in the UK, have become camera-mad! We have cameras in places we don't expect them and certainly don't need them! The whole country's camera-crazy but I think we just don't notice them anymore.
Host	And what are these places where we don't expect or need them?
Herald	Schools and hospitals, for example. These places are full of people with eyes in their heads! Why do we need cameras?
Host	Well, we've heard two very opposing views now, so Johnny Pitt, you spend a lot of time in front of cameras. Do you also like them to watch you in the street when you're going about your daily business?
Pitt	Well, I guess I find it normal to see cameras everywhere. The world is a dangerous place and I think that if people know there's a good chance that there's a camera recording them, they'll think twice before breaking the law. Privacy is of course important but I'm willing to lose some of it to stay safe if it reduces crime.
Host	Megan O'Hara, you represent the UK's student community. What do you think about the importance of personal safety and privacy?
O'Hara	I want safety *and* privacy. I don't agree that it's a question of one or the other. There was personal safety before we had cameras everywhere and now we have more and more cameras and less and less personal safety. As for privacy, we can forget it! Not only do we have surveillance cameras recording our every move, whistleblowers now tell us that hackers can secretly turn on our mobile phone cameras, so how do we know the police aren't doing this, as well? I also don't agree with Johnny Pitt that cameras will make people think twice before breaking the law. Cameras may help the police *after* a crime but they don't *stop* crimes.
Host	Would you like to comment on that Detective Inspector Langton?
Inspector	The police don't break the law, Ms O'Hara! We defend it and we use all legal methods to protect citizens of this country, no more and no less.
O'Hara	Oh really! It didn't look like that at our last student demonstration when the police …
Host	Let's stick to the point, please. Sally Herald, do you agree that cameras can prevent crimes?
Herald	Well, I certainly don't agree with Johnny Pitt on that point. We all remember that picture of him punching a photographer outside his hotel, so I don't think he thinks twice before breaking the law!
Pitt	That was self-defence! The guy was in my way and wouldn't move. It just looked like a punch!
Herald	That's not what the doctor said at the hospital! I interviewed him personally and he said he thought the photographer had been hit by a boxer. I'm sure you were making a boxing movie at the time …

Host	I think it's time to hear our listeners' comments. We have a tweet from …

Unit 14, Exercise 3

Jenny Wade	I think it's crazy to take any more fossil fuels out of the ground when we know that climate change is getting out of control. Now, what we need to do is to invest everything in renewable forms of energy. That way, we'll have a chance of saving the world for our children and grandchildren.
Stella King	I'm really worried about the noise, with big trucks going along our narrow roads at all hours, day and night. And think how dangerous it will be for us all – especially for our children. We mustn't allow this development to take place.
Lyn Benson	It probably won't be easy for the community for a while, that's for sure. But they're promising to put a lot of money into the community in return, and that will do some real good for all of us far into the future.
Brian Fox	I'm old enough to remember times when the lights went out, and it wasn't nice. We've already closed down a lot of the old coal-fired power stations, and it'll be years before renewables can replace them. And gas is a lot cleaner than coal, so we should use that to keep the lights on for the next 20 years.
Alan Smith	Why should we support this fracking project? It doesn't make any sense, does it? I mean, this is the sort of thing that'll give a lot more money to people who already have a lot of money. And what do we local people get in return? Nothing – nothing but trouble!
Bob Lowe	I think we should welcome this development even if it means accepting some noise and a bit of a hard time for a few months. Remember: after those few months, production will continue year after year without any more problems. That seems all right to me – especially as I may be able to get a job!

Unit 15, Exercise 5A

So you're hungry, but let's say you've only got £10 to spend. What will you buy – fast food or fresh food to cook for yourselves?

Well, if you go to your local fast-food restaurant, it's all very simple. You'll be able to get two burgers that cost £2.40 each for a total of £4.80. With those, of course, you'll want two portions of French fries and they'll cost you another £3.20. After that, well, you need something to drink and two medium colas will cost £1.80. Is there enough for any extras – fruit yogurts, perhaps? Well,

no, because you've already spent £9.80 on your rather basic dinner for two.

Now, if you go to the supermarket, you'll get more for your money. For two portions of chicken, you'll need to pay £3.10. Half a kilo of potatoes will be yours for just 60 pence. Then allow £3.80 for some healthy salad vegetables. You can get some fruit, too, for another £1.20. And finally, you can get a litre of milk for just 90 pence. Total: £9.60 and you've got yourselves a good, healthy dinner for two that won't leave you hungry in the middle of the night!

Unit 15, Exercise 5B

So why does anyone choose fast food? Well, they might prefer to eat fast food for various reasons. First of all, some people just love this sort of food. After all, these big fast-food chains do a lot of research on creating food that's tasty – food that people want to come back for again and again. Secondly, there are also lots of people who really don't like cooking very much. It's too much of a chore, and they're more interested in their work or in other things. Thirdly, these days there are other people who really don't know how to cook. They just never learned, perhaps because their own parents were too busy to teach them. And finally, of course, fast food is what it says it is: fast. In today's busy world, a lot of people have to rush round all the time – perhaps between two different jobs, for example. For them, fast food just takes less time and trouble than a home-cooked meal.

Unit 15, Exercise 5C

So just how much time and trouble do these different types of meal take? Well, let's think about your local fast-food restaurant first. Let's say going there and back takes 15 minutes. Then when you're there, you have to order what you want and then wait for a short time, so let's say ordering takes five minutes. And after that, there's just the eating, and it isn't a very big meal, is it? So let's say eating takes another 15 minutes. That's a total of 35 minutes and you're all done.

But now what about the home-cooked meal? Well first you've got to go and get everything from the shop and then get home again. So let's say shopping takes 45 minutes. Then there's preparing the food – washing the vegetables, cooking and so on. So let's allow another 45 minutes for preparing. Now comes the good bit – eating! Well, you've got quite a big meal, so that should take another 20 minutes. Then, finally, there's washing up and tidying up to do after that. Not so nice, but very important. And let's allow 15 minutes for that. That's a total of 125 minutes all together. Over two hours in other words!

Unit 16, Exercise 4

Mark Moro	Now let's open the debate about driverless cars to our studio audience. First, please, the lady in the green jacket.
Sylvia Ray	Thank you. I'm Sylvia Ray and I'm an A & E nurse. Every day I see the horrible results of road accidents – accidents

usually caused by human error. So I'm in favour of this new technology. It seems to me that driverless cars have the potential to cut the number of deaths and injuries on the roads. We don't have as many emergency service staff and doctors and nurses as we need, and you know what? Thanks to driverless cars, we'll now be released to handle more of the other medical problems we're trained to deal with.

Mark Moro   Thank you. All right, well now let's hear from the man in the grey suit.

Ben Miller   I'm Ben Miller. I'm the Director of Right Road Construction and, as you might expect, I think driverless cars are a terrible idea! If they can really drive very close together, that means we'll never need to build any more roads. That'll cut the need for the work my organization does – road construction. The only thing anyone will want us for is to repair the roads and bridges we've already got. Thinking about the whole road construction industry, that'll cost lots of jobs. I don't want to see that.

Mark Moro   Thank you. So we've now had one view in favour and one view very much against driverless cars. Now the young lady in the yellow blouse.

Julie North   Thank you. Well, I'm Julie North and I'm a car insurance salesperson, and from a personal point of view I'm against driverless cars. If they really and truly mean a much higher level of safety, then that will bring down the amount drivers have to pay for their car insurance. And that can only mean one thing: many of the people selling car insurance like me will have to start again – maybe training to sell other sorts of insurance instead.

Mark Moro   Thank you. Well, I can see that would be a problem for some people, though a lot more people would be very happy to see the cost of driving come down like that. All right, let's have one more opinion now. The man in the blue jacket, please.

Peter Hill   I'm Peter Hill. I'm a city planning officer, and I have to say that I'm very much in favour of this new technology. I want our cities to work more efficiently, and one of the really inefficient things is the way traffic moves – or doesn't move. A lot of the time, cars are parked on roads or in great big car parks. Now driverless cars will be shared by lots of people, and so that problem will mostly disappear because these cars won't need to be parked for long. As soon as one person has driven into the city centre, for example, the car can be called to someone else. It'll drive straight there, pick up the next person and drive to the next place.